America's Secret Recipes 1

RON DOUGLAS

Make Your Favorite Restaurant Dishes at Home

Copyright © 2009, Verity Associates, LLC
All rights reserved

RecipeSecrets.net and Verity Associates, LLC are not sponsored, endorsed, or affiliated with any recipe source. We disclaim using any copyright or trademark.

This document is a compilation of recipes and cooking tips based on personal interpretation of the foods listed. Through trial and error, each recipe was created to taste the same as, or similar to, its restaurant/brand counterpart, but they are not the actual recipes used by the manufacturer or creator.

The brand or restaurant names for the recipes have only been included as an aid in cataloging the recipes and do not imply authenticity or endorsement by the manufacturer or creator. All restaurant and company names are trademarks of their respective owners. Please see our Trademarks section towards the end of this cookbook for detailed trademark credits.

All information provided through this cookbook is intended to be accurate. However, there may be inaccuracies at times which we will make every attempt to correct when found. Some of the information provided may be intended to assist you in making decisions but does not eliminate the need to discuss your particular circumstances with a qualified professional.

For the actual and authentic version of the food products listed in this compilation, please patronize the individual restaurant or manufacturer.

To the best of the author's knowledge, all company related information and trademark details are true and accurate. Any misrepresentation of factual material is unintentional.

No part of this publication may be reproduced, stored in or introduced into a retrieval system, or transmitted in any form, or by any means (electronic, mechanical, photocopying, recording, or otherwise), without the prior written permission of both the author and copyright owner.

Printed in the United States of America

Published and distributed by: Verity Associates, LLC
                                 PO Box 670361
                                 Kew Gardens Hills, NY 11367

To all the friends I've made at RecipeSecrets.net over the years, thanks for your inspiration and contributions to this cookbook.

To Nia and Ryan - if this world were mine, I'd give it all to you.

To all readers - You're Invited!... Come share recipes and good times with us online at:

www.RecipeSecrets.net/forums

PREFACE

I've always been a "Foodie" but I never expected that my cooking hobby would ever lead to anything other than happy guests at the dinner table. I guess destiny had other plans for my culinary passion.

I stumbled upon my quest into "recipe cloning" on a cold and rainy day in late 2002 when my wife and I had a craving for KFC chicken. Being that the weather was so bad, we decided to try to make our own version at home. As I was searching the Internet for the recipe, I discovered that there were many people on the message boards also looking for restaurant recipes. However, there weren't many places to find quality recipes that actually worked. Having been in ecommerce at the time, I saw this as a golden opportunity.

In 2003, and friend and I started RecipeSecrets.net - a community website featuring our version of popular restaurant recipes. The site was a big hit and started getting a lot of visitors in a short period of time. It became many people's favorite place online to share clone restaurant recipes. Today RecipeSecrets.net gets over 1 million views per month.

To keep in contact with all the members of the site, in 2004 we started "The Recipe Secrets Newsletter." Each week my partner and I would try to replicate a new dish from a popular chain restaurant like The Cheesecake Factory, The Olive Garden, T.G.I. Friday's etc. We would then feature the "secret recipe" in the email newsletter and ask for feedback.

Through years of trial and error and with the help of our subscribers, we perfected the collection clone recipes featured in this cookbook. Each recipe has been tested and tweaked to taste just like the original.

These are the "secret recipes" which are generating billions of dollars for the restaurant industry every year. Now you can save money and impress your friends by preparing them in your own kitchen!

Due to intellectual property laws, we can only claim to offer "clones" of these famous dishes. However, we're confident that if you follow these instructions, you won't be able to tell the difference.

We encourage you to put the book to good use and make these famous dishes yourself. Once you've tried the recipes, you'll see what makes them so special and why we have so many satisfied customers.

We also invite you to interact with our online community and get thousands of additional recipes on "The Secret Recipe Forum" - go to: www.RecipeSecrets.net/forum.

I hope this cookbook brings enjoyment for you, your family and friends for years to come.

Ron Douglas

CONTENTS

Continued on next page

Applebee's Broiled Salmon with Garlic Butter

Description: *Salmon filets broiled just right with melted butter and a hint of garlic.*

Ingredients

4 (5 ounce) salmon filets
melted butter, as needed
pepper, to taste
garlic powder, to taste
salt, to taste
garlic butter, as needed

RecipeSecrets.net tip:
Make your own garlic butter using softened butter and fresh minced garlic.

1. Preheat grill or heavy skillet to 550 degrees F.

2. In small pan, melt butter. Brush raw salmon filets with melted butter; sprinkle with salt, pepper and garlic powder. Do this to both sides. Discard any remaining melted butter - it cannot be used for anything. Place brush in hot soapy water and clean thoroughly. Rinse well.

3. Place salmon in hot skillet or on grill and cook approximately 2 minutes; turn carefully and continue to cook an additional 2 to 3 minutes or until cooked through.

4. Remove from heat; with clean brush (after it has been thoroughly washed and rinsed) lightly brush with garlic butter made from softened butter and fresh minced garlic (or garlic powder, if preferred). Serve hot.

Serves 4

About Applebee's:

Applebee's® was founded in Atlanta, Georgia, by Bill and T.J. Palmer. They envisioned a restaurant that would provide full service, consistently good food, reasonable prices and quality service in a neighbor-hood setting. Their first restaurant,T.J. Applebee's Rx for Edibles & Elixirs®, opened in November 1980.

Applebee's Caramel Appletini

Description: *Like sipping on a caramel apple. A sweet blend of vodka, red apple liqueur and caramel syrup - garnished with fresh apple.*

Ingredients

1oz Shakka Red Apple Liqueur®
1oz Stoli Vanilla®
1 oz Monin Caramel Syrup®
2 oz apple juice
1 oz caramel
apple slices, for garnish

1. In shaker, combine red apple liqueur, Stoli vanilla, apple juice and caramel syrup; shake well to blend.
2. Pour 1-ounce of caramel in the bottom of a martini glass; pour contents from shaker over top. Garnish with an apple slice. Serve.

Serves 1

RecipeSecrets.net tip: Caramel syrup adds taste and excitement to coffee, latte`s, soda`s and cocktails.

Applebee's Lemonade

Description: *Refreshingly delicious lemonade.*

Ingredients

1 quart water
1 cup sugar
1 cup fresh squeezed lemon juice
sparkling water (not tonic water)
mint leaves, for garnish

1. Combine water, sugar and lemon juice; blend well.
2. Fill a tall glass 2/3 to the top with lemon mixture; fill glass with sparkling water.
3. Garnish with mint leaf; serve.

Serves 4

RecipeSecrets.net tip: Use your favorite artificial sweetener in place of sugar for a healthy alternative.

Applebee's Orange Creamsicle Cake

Description: *A creamy and delectable cream cheese filling topped with a blend of smooth orange cream - just like the creamsicles we all enjoy.*

Ingredients

Graham Cracker Crust:
1/2 cups graham cracker crumbs
1/4 cup granulated sugar
5 tablespoons melted butter

Cheese Cake:
1 (8 ounce) package cream
  cheese, at room temperature
1/2 cup sour cream, room
  temperature
1/4 cup granulated sugar
2 eggs

Jell-O Mandarin Orange Topping:
2 boxes orange flavor Jell-O
3 tablespoons sugar

2 cups hot water
1/2 cup mandarin orange puree
pieces of pound cake
pieces of mandarin oranges

Orange Cream:
1 (8 ounce) package cream
  cheese, softened
2 cups mandarin orange puree
2 cups heavy (whipping) cream

Whipped Cream Topping:
1 cup heavy (whipping) cream
1/4 cup sugar
1/2 teaspoon vanilla

1. Preheat oven to 350 degrees F.
2. Prepare crust: In bowl, combine graham cracker crumbs and sugar; drizzle with melted butter; mix well. Press onto the bottom and sides of 9-inch baking pan; set aside.
3. Prepare cheesecake filling: In medium bowl, beat softened cream cheese until very light; add sour cream; sprinkle sugar over while beating creams together; beat in sugar until well-blended.
4. Add eggs, one at a time, beating well after each addition. Spread over crust.
5. Place in preheated oven and bake 15 to 20 minutes

or until cheesecake is done. Allow to cool on wire rack.

6. Prepare Orange Topping: In medium bowl, dissolve Jell-O in 2 cups hot water, stirring to dissolve completely. Stir in mandarin orange puree; blend well; pour over cheesecake. Place in refrigerator to cool. Before Jell-O sets, press pieces of pound cake and pieces of mandarin oranges into the Jell-O, leaving some of the pieces sticking out of the Jell-O. Chill until set.

7. Prepare Orange Cream: In medium bowl, beat cream cheese until very light and fluffy. Drain canned mandarin oranges and remove any membranes; transfer to blender; puree until smooth. Add mandarin puree and heavy cream to cream cheese; beat until well incorporated. Spread over set Jell-O. Return to refrigerator. Chill.

8. Prepare Whipped Cream topping: In medium bowl, with clean beaters, whip heavy cream with sugar and vanilla just until soft peaks form. Spread over Orange Cream; return to refrigerator.

Serves 8

A note on cheesecakes:

When done baking, a perfectly baked cheesecake will be puffed around the edges. The center should still be slightly moist and will jiggle. Look at the edges of your cheesecake and you will see tiny cracks. As your cheesecake cools, the cracks will seal together. Cheesecakes become firmer as they cool. It is best to refrigerate at least 8 hours or overnight before serving.

Applebee's Santa Fe Chicken Salad

Description: *Salad with a Southwestern flair. Crispy greens with marinated fajita-seasoned chicken strips and the crunch of tortilla chips served with pico de gallo, sour cream and guacamole.*

Ingredients

1 boneless chicken breast
mixed salad greens
crushed tortilla chips
sour cream
guacamole

Pico de Gallo:
3 large tomatoes, diced
1 large onion, diced
2 tablespoons jalapenos, diced
2 teaspoons salt
1/2 teaspoon freshly-ground
  black pepper
1/2 teaspoon garlic powder
1/2 cup fresh cilantro, chopped
1 tablespoon olive oil
1 tablespoon white vinegar

Marinade:
2 tablespoons gold tequila
1/4 cup freshly squeezed lime
  juice
2 tablespoons freshly squeezed
  orange juice
1 teaspoon fajita seasoning mix
3/4 teaspoon minced fresh
  jalapeno pepper (seeded)

3/4 teaspoon minced fresh garlic
1/4 teaspoon kosher salt
1/4 teaspoon fresh ground black
  pepper

Mexi-Ranch Dressing:
1/4 cup mayonnaise
1/4 cup sour cream
1 tablespoon milk
2 teaspoons minced tomato
1/2 teaspoon white vinegar
1 teaspoon minced canned
  jalapeno slices
1 teaspoon minced onion
1/4 teaspoon dried parsley
1/4 teaspoon Tabasco pepper
  sauce
1/8 teaspoon salt
1/8 teaspoon dried dill weed
1/8 teaspoon paprika
1/8 teaspoon cayenne pepper
1/8 teaspoon cumin
1/8 teaspoon chili powder
1 dash garlic powder
1 dash freshly-ground black
  pepper

1. Prepare Pico de Gallo: In small bowl, combine all ingredients; mix well; cover and refrigerate overnight.

2. Place all marinade ingredients in resealable plastic bag or in non-reactive baking pan; add chicken, turn to coat. If using a pan, cover. Refrigerate over night, turning chicken in marinade occasionally.

3. When ready to cook chicken, preheat grill. Remove chicken from marinade; discard marinade. Season both sides of chicken with fajita seasoning. Place on hot grill and grill until done and juices run clear.

4. Meanwhile, prepare Mexi-Ranch Dressing: In small bowl, combine all ingredients and mix well. Cover and refrigerate.

5. Prepare a plate of your favorite greens. Place a ramekin or sour cream, a ramekin of pico de gallo and a ramekin of guacamole on plate. Top salad with chicken.

6. Garnish with chopped scallions and crushed tortilla chips. Serve with Applebee's Mexi-Ranch Dressing.

Serves 1

Applebee's Tijuana "Philly" Steak Sandwich

Description: *The traditional philly sandwich done with Southwestern flair.*

Ingredients

1 mushroom diced
1 tablespoon butter softened
1/2 teaspoon salt
3 oz Steak-Umm
1/4 cup shredded Cheddar cheese
1/4 cup shredded Monterey Jack cheese
1 flour tortilla - (10" dia)

1 tablespoon diced tomato
1 teaspoon diced red onion
1/4 teaspoon finely-chopped fresh cilantro
1 slice bacon cooked

1. In small saute pan, saute mushrooms in ½ teaspoon butter; season lightly with salt and pepper.

2. In separate skillet, fry beef, breaking into pieces; fry until done; drain; season with salt and pepper.

3. Meanwhile, sprinkle blend of cheeses in center of tortilla; top with tomato, onion, mushroom and cilantro. Crumble bacon and sprinkle over top. Top with beef; add additional salt and pepper, if desired.

4. Bring sides of tortilla up and fold in burrito style. Butter top and bottom of sandwich.

5. Grill over medium heat, making sure pan is nice and hot. Grill 2 minutes per side.

6. To serve: Slice in half diagonally. Serve with lettuce, sour cream and salsa.

Serves 1

Aunt Jemima Maple Syrup

Description: *The famous flavor of an all-time favorite - made right in your own kitchen.*

Ingredients

2 cups water
1 cup granulated sugar
2 cups dark corn syrup
1/4 teaspoon salt
1 teaspoon maple flavoring

RecipeSecrets.net tip:
Making a quart at home is half the price of one bottle from your local grocery store.

1. In heavy, medium saucepan, combine water, sugar, corn syrup and salt. Over medium heat, stir occasionally, until mixture comes to a full boil. Let boil for 7 minutes.
2. Turn off heat; cool for 15 minutes.
3. Add maple flavoring, stirring well to combine.
4. When completely cool, transfer to plastic container or glass bottle with cover. Refrigerate.

Makes 1 quart.

About Aunt Jemima:

Just hearing "Aunt Jemima"® makes everyone think of breakfast foods, pancakes, waffles and this delicious syrup.

B.B. King's Blues Club and Restaurant Southern Style Catfish

Description: *Simple to make, with a nice, mild flavor. Just add some coleslaw and fries for a complete meal.*

Ingredients

2 cups white cornmeal
2 tablespoons salt
1 tablespoon pepper
2 (6 ounce) catfish fillets, washed well
coleslaw, French fries and hushpuppies as accompaniments

RecipeSecrets.net tip: Substitute cod, pollock, rainbow trout or striped bass for the catfish.

1. Heat peanut oil in deep fryer to 350 degrees F.
2. In shallow dish or pie pan, combine cornmeal, salt and pepper; blend well. Dredge wet catfish in mixture, pressing to coat well on both sides; shake off excess.
3. Carefully place catfish in hot oil. Fry 6 to 8 minutes, or until catfish is brown and crispy; remove to rack or paper towels to drain.
4. Serve with coleslaw, French fries and hushpuppies.

Serves 2

About B.B. King's Blues Club & Restaurant:

B.B. King's® Blues Club & Restaurant is a cross between the nightclub experience and a nice restaurant. It's a great place to get dinner and hear some great music.

Bahama Breeze Grilled Fish Tostada Salad

Description: *Creole seasoned fresh fish over crisp flour tortillas with three cheeses, field greens with tropical vinaigrette, tomato salsa, chimichurri sauce and avocado.*

Ingredients

4 six-ounce fresh fish fillets
1 teaspoon Creole seasoning
½ teaspoon kosher salt
8 small flour tortillas
12 ounces finely shredded
  cheese (Mexican blend)
6 cups spring mix of lettuce,
  washed, dried and torn
½ cup Citrus Vinaigrette (recipe
  follows)
½ cup cooked corn kernels
4 ounces sliced roasted peppers
  (red, yellow or poblano)
8 ounces Tomato Salsa (recipe
  follows)
¼ cup Chimichurri Sauce (recipe
  follows)
1 ripe avocado, quartered and
  cut into fan

Citrus Vinaigrette:
2 tablespoons extra virgin olive
  oil
2/3 cup rice wine vinegar
1/3 cup orange juice
1 tablespoon Dijon mustard
1 teaspoon honey
2 teaspoons minced fresh garlic
1 tablespoon minced shallots
  (onion may be substituted)
1/2 teaspoon Creole seasoning
2 tablespoons chopped fresh
  cilantro

Tomato Salsa:
1 ½ lbs. plum tomatoes, seeded
  and diced
½ cup finely diced red onion
  (you may use white or yellow)
2 cloves garlic, minced
2 tablespoons chopped fresh
  cilantro or 2 teaspoons dried
2 teaspoons finely diced fresh
  jalapeno (1 pepper)
1 teaspoon Creole seasoning
Kosher salt, to taste
juice of one lime (bottled lime
  juice can be used)
2 tablespoons extra virgin olive
  oil

Chimichurri Sauce:
3/4 cup extra virgin olive oil
1/3 cup rice wine vinegar
1/2 cup fresh squeezed lemon
  juice
2 teaspoons kosher salt
1/2 teaspoon black pepper
1 bunch (1 ½ ounces) flat-leaf
  parsley, stemmed and minced
1/2 bunch (½ ounce) cilantro,
  stemmed and minced
1/2 teaspoon dried oregano
scallion tops, thinly sliced
4 teaspoons minced garlic

1. Prepare Citrus Vinaigrette: In small bowl, combine olive oil, vinegar, orange juice, mustard, honey, garlic, shallots, Creole seasoning and cilantro: blend well; cover and refrigerate until ready to use.
2. Prepare Tomato Salsa: In small bowl, combine all ingredients; blend well; cover and refrigerate until ready to use.
3. Prepare Chimichurri Sauce: In small bowl, combine olive oil, vinegar, lemon juice, salt and pepper; whisking until well blended. Add parsley, cilantro, oregano, garlic and scallions; using a rubber spatula mix gently until well blended.
4. Preheat oven to 375 degrees F. Preheat grill.
5. Season fish with Creole seasoning and kosher salt-coating both sides.
6. Grill until well-done (the internal temperature of the-fish should read 145 degrees F. on meat thermometer when inserted). Remove from grill.
7. Meanwhile, lay tortilla shells in single layer on baking-sheet. Using a fork, poke holes over entire shell about ½-inch apart. Brush lightly with oil and bake in preheated oven until lightly brown - about 5 minutes.
8. Sprinkle each shell evenly with cheese; return to oven and bake until cheese is melted completely.
9. Divide the tortillas among 4 plates.
10. Toss spring mix with vinaigrette, corn kernels, and peppers; divide among the 4 plates. Sprinkle Tomato Salsa over salad mix. Slice fish fillets and place on top of salsa; drizzle with Chimichurra sauce. Top each with an avocado fan.

Serves 4

About Bahama Breeze:

Bahama Breeze® is an American restaurant specializing in Caribbean inspired fresh seafood, chicken and steaks. Founded in Orlando, Florida in 1996, there are over 2 dozen locations throughout the states.

Bailey's Original Irish Cream

Description: *That fine combination of Irish-tasting whiskey and cream-based liqueur. Drink as it is, over ice or as part of a cocktail.*

Ingredients

1 cup light cream
1 can Eagle Brand sweetened condensed milk (14 oz.)
1 2/3 cups Irish whiskey
1 teaspoon instant coffee
2 tablespoons Hershey's chocolate syrup
1 teaspoon vanilla extract
1 teaspoon almond extract

1. Place ingredients in blender; blend at high speed for 30 seconds.
2. Transfer to bottle with a tight seal; refrigerate. The liqueur will keep for at least 2 months if kept cool. Be sure to shake the bottle well before serving.

Makes 4 cups.

Balducci's Tiramisu

Description: *An Italian masterpiece. This stunning dessert features delicate lady fingers dipped in espresso coffee and covered with an airy filling of whipped mascarpone and flavored just perfectly.*

Ingredients

24 ladyfingers, toasted in a 375 degree F oven for 15 minutes
2 cups espresso coffee, cooled
6 eggs, separated
3 to 6 tablespoons granulated sugar, to taste
1 pound mascarpone

2 tablespoons Marsala wine
2 tablespoons Triple Sec
2 tablespoons brandy
2 tablespoons orange extract
8 ounces bittersweet chocolate, finely chopped

RecipeSecrets.net tip: Substitute cream cheese for the mascarpone in this recipe.

1. Arrange ladyfingers on plate and sprinkle with cooled espresso. Place half the ladyfingers in single layer in a rectangular serving dish.

2. In medium bowl, beat the egg yolks with sugar until yolks turn pale in color. Add mascarpone, liquors and extract stirring gently to blend.

3. In separate bowl, beat egg whites vigorously with wire whisk until stiff. Gently fold whites into mascarpone mixture. Spread half this mixture over ladyfingers; sprinkle with half the chopped chocolate. Repeat layering, starting with remaining soaked ladyfingers.

4. Cover with foil and refrigerate at least 1 hour before serving.

Serves 8

About Balducci's:

Balducci's® is a unique market with restaurant-quality prepared foods. They currently have 10 stores on the U.S. East Coast.

Ben & Jerry's Cherry Garcia Recipe

Description: *The first ice cream named for a rock star. This blend of flavors is a real treat for the taste buds.*

Ingredients

1/4 cup shaved semi-sweet chocolate bars
1/4 cup fresh Bing cherries, halved and pitted (if canned cherries are used, drain the syrup)
2 large eggs
3/4 cup sugar
2 cups heavy or whipping cream
1 cup milk

1. Place shaved chocolate flakes in small bowl. Place cherries in separate small bowl; cover both and refrigerate.
2. In medium bowl, whisk eggs until light and fluffy, 1 to 2 minutes; gradually whisk in sugar until completely blended, another minute or so. Add cream and milk; whisk to blend.
3. Transfer mixture to ice cream maker and freeze according to manufacturer's instructions.
4. When the ice cream begins to thicken (about 2 minutes before it is done), stir in chocolate and cherries; continue freezing until ice cream is done.

Serves 4

About Ben & Jerry's:

Ben & Jerry's® was founded in Vermont in 1978. They are known for their innovative flavors and fresh ingredients.

Benihana's Ginger Salad Dressing

Description: *Prepare your favorite salad and splash on this flavorful dressing for a unique taste.*

Ingredients

1/2 cup minced onion
1/2 cup peanut oil
1/3 cup rice vinegar
2 tablespoons water
2 tablespoons minced fresh
  ginger
2 tablespoons minced celery
2 tablespoons ketchup
4 teaspoons soy sauce

2 teaspoons sugar
2 teaspoons fresh lemon juice
1/2 teaspoon minced garlic
1/2 teaspoon salt
1/4 teaspoon black pepper

1. Place all ingredients in blender; blend on high speed for 30 seconds or until the ginger is well-pureed and mixture is well blended.
2. Store in covered container in refrigerator.

Makes 1 3/4 cups.

About Benihana:

Benihana® started out as a tiny four-table restaurant in New York City's theater district before becoming an international chain. Diners sit around large tables where chefs ostentatiously chop, slice, stir-fry and grill.

Black Eyed Pea Cornbread

Description: *The old fashioned goodness of Southern-made corn-bread.*

Ingredients

1 lb. ground beef
1 cup canned black-eyed peas, drained
1 cup onion, chopped
3/4 cup cream-style corn
1 cup cornmeal
1/2 cup flour

1 cup buttermilk
1/4 cup cooking oil
2 eggs, slightly beaten
1 teaspoon salt
1/2 teaspoon baking soda
2 jalapeno peppers, chopped
1 cup Cheddar cheese, grated

1. Preheat oven to 350 degrees F. Grease 13 X 9 X 2-inch baking pan; set aside.
2. In skillet, over medium-high heat, brown meat; drain well. Break into small pieces.
3. Add remaining ingredients to skillet; mix well.
4. Remove from heat and transfer to prepared baking pan.
5. Bake in preheated oven for 45 minutes, or until done.

Serves 6

About Black Eyed Pea:

Black Eyed Pea® was founded in 1975 by Gene Street in Dallas, Texas and eventually expanded across the southern United States. Their menu features home-style Southern cuisine - catfish, chicken fried steak, mashed potatoes, fried okra, cornbread and rolls. Their signature dish - "black eyed peas."

Bob Evans Cinnamon-Raisin Biscuits

Description: *A warm, cinnamon-flavored biscuit studded with raisins and topped with white glaze.*

Ingredients

1 2/3 cups all-purpose flour
1 1/2 cups sifted cake flour
1/4 cup granulated sugar
1 tablespoon baking powder
1 teaspoon salt
1 1/2 teaspoons ground
  cinnamon
1/2 cup plus 1 tablespoon butter
  or margarine

1 cup raisins
1 cup plus 1 to 2 tablespoons
  milk, divided use
melted margarine (for brushing
  tops)
1 cup sifted confectioners' sugar

1. Preheat oven to 400 degrees F. Grease baking sheets; set aside.
2. In large bowl, combine flour, sugar, baking powder, salt and cinnamon; whisk to combine.   Using a pastry blender or 2 knives, cut in ½ cup plus 1 tablespoon butter or margarine until mixture resembles coarse meal. Add raisins and 1 cup milk.
3. Stir, using wooden spoon, until moistened (do not over mix).
4. Turn dough out onto floured surface and lightly knead 10 times; roll dough to a ¾-inch thickness; cut with a 2-inch biscuit cutter. Transfer to prepared baking sheets and brush tops lightly with melted butter or margarine.
5. Place in preheated oven; bake 15 minutes or until golden.
6. Prepare glaze: In small bowl, combine 1 cup confectioners' sugar with 1 to 2 tablespoons milk; stir until smooth.
7. While still warm, drizzle with glaze.

Makes 16 biscuits.

Bob Evans Stuffed Caramel Banana Pecan Cream Pancakes

Description: *Pancakes baked with pecans and sliced fresh bananas, covered in a warm, caramel sauce.*

Ingredients

2 cups prepared vanilla pudding
2 cups cream cheese, room
  temperature
prepared pancake batter for 2
  pancakes
2 tablespoons honey roasted
  pecans
1 banana sliced into 1/2-inch
  thick slices

caramel sauce
1 tablespoon powdered sugar
whipped topping

RecipeSecrets.net tip:
Be sure to let the pecans
and bananas show for a
nice presentation.

1. Mix vanilla pudding with cream cheese until blended and creamy, no lumps. Cover and refrigerate. This mixture can store, covered, in the refrigerator for up to 5 days.

2. Prepare pancake batter and preheat griddle. Ladle batter onto hot griddle and sprinkle evenly with pecans and banana slices. When they bubble and edges are dry, flip to cook second side.

3. When done, place pancake on plate, top with 4 tablespoons Vanilla Cream Cheese mixture and top with second pancake. Ladle with caramel sauce and sprinkle with confectioners' sugar. Garnish with whipped topping.

Serves 1

Bob's Big Boy Hamburger

Description: *Enjoy your own version of this famous double cheeseburger with special sauce.*

Ingredients

1 pound ground chuck beef
8 jumbo sesame seed buns
1 cup shredded lettuce
4 slices real American cheese
Big Boy sauce *(see page 23)*
salt

1. Preheat grill.
2. Form beef into eight 4-inch patties; grill one side and season with salt; turn; season and grill second side.

RecipeSecrets.net tip:
For a healthy alternative, try preparing this recipe with ground chicken or turkey

2. Prepare rolls by discarding 4 Crowns (save for making bread crumbs, stuffing or croutons). Toast remaining 4 crowns and the 8 heels until golden.

3. Spread Big Boy sauce on all 8 heels and add lettuce to each heel. Place a slice of cheese on top of lettuce on 4 of the heels.

4. Place one patty on each heel. Stack heels without cheese on top of heels with cheese and top each with toasted crowns.

Serves 4

About Bob's Big Boy:

Big Boy® started as Bob's Pantry in Glendale California by Bob Wian. They focus on quality food and great service.

Bob's Big Boy Hamburger Sauce

Description: *A delicious sauce for burgers and sandwiches.*

Ingredients

1 cup mayonnaise
1/4 cup bottled chili sauce
1/4 cup ketchup
3 tablespoons sugar
1/2 cup pickle relish undrained
dash garlic salt

*RecipeSecrets.net tip:
For a healthy alternative, use fat-free or low-fat mayonnaise and sugar substitute.*

1. Place ingredients in small bowl; mix until well combined.
2. Store in covered container in refrigerator.
3. Use this sauce on burgers and sandwiches; will keep for up to a week in the refrigerator, covered.

Makes 2 cups.

Bob's Big Boy Slim Jim Sandwich

Description: *An easily made ham and cheese grilled sandwich with lettuce, tomato and dressing.*

Ingredients

6 ounces thinly sliced Virginia
  baked ham
3 ounces thinly sliced natural
  Swiss cheese
1 (6 or 8-inch) hoagie or
  sub-style sandwich roll
4 thin tomato slices
shredded lettuce

Thousand Island dressing
1 tablespoon butter or
  margarine, softened

RecipeSecrets.net tip:
Use Big Boy Hamburger
sauce from page 23 in place
of Thousand Island dress-
ing.

1. Preheat grill.
2. Butter split rolls and place on grill to toast until lightly browned. Remove from grill/griddle and assemble sandwich: Heel of bun, ham, cheese, lettuce, tomato, Big Boy Sauce or Thousand Island dressing on inside of crown.
3. Place assembled sandwich on grill; press down with heavy metal or cast iron pan; grill until cheese melts.
4. Serve with French fries and dill pickle spears on the side.

Serves 1

Bull's Eye Barbecue Sauce

Description: *Smokey, sweet BBQ sauce for all your favorite bar-becue recipes.*

Ingredients

1 cup Heinz ketchup
6 tablespoons Lea & Perrins Worcestershire Sauce
4 tablespoons butter
3 tablespoons distilled white vinegar
1 tablespoon French's yellow mustard
3 tablespoons finely minced yellow onion

4 teaspoons hickory flavor liquid smoke
1/4 teaspoon Tabasco sauce
1/2 cup brown sugar, firmly packed
1 tablespoon granulated white sugar
1 teaspoon table salt

RecipeSecrets.net tip: The hickory flavor liquid smoke really adds to this recipes flavor.

1. In saucepan, over very low heat, combine all ingredients; mix well to blend.

2. Bring to simmer and simmer 15 minutes, stirring occasionally.

3. Cool; store in covered container in refrigerator. You can use a clean an old BBQ sauce bottle, or a ketchup bottle.

Makes 2 cups of sauce.

Cajun Cafe's Bourbon Chicken

Description: *A tangy, boneless chicken dish marinated and smothered in bourbon sauce.*

Ingredients

1 pound chicken leg or thigh
  meat cut in bite size chunks
4 ounces soy sauce
1/2 cup brown sugar, firmly
  packed
1/2 teaspoon garlic powder

1 teaspoon powdered ginger
2 tablespoons dried minced
  onion
1/2 cup Jim Beam bourbon
  whiskey
2 tablespoons white wine

1. Place chicken in glass bowl or baking pan.
2. In small bowl, combine all marinade ingredients (except 2 tablespoons wine); mix well; pour over chicken to coat; turn chicken pieces to coat well.
3. Cover and refrigerate for several hours, turning chicken occasionally. If using baking pan, make sure chicken is in single layer.
4. When ready to cook, preheat oven to 350 degrees F. Place baking pan in preheated oven; bake and baste every 10 minutes until cooked through, about 1 hour.
5. When done, remove chicken to serving platter; keep warm. Scrape pan juices with all the browned bits into skillet; heat; add 2 tablespoons white wine. Stir and add chicken. Cook for 1 minute and serve.

Serves 4

California Pizza Kitchen Roasted Garlic Paste

Description: *This can be used in pasta dishes, mashed potatoes, salads, and more. Mix with a little olive oil and toss with hot cooked pasta: top with Parmesan cheese.*

Ingredients

2/3 cup coarsely chopped garlic
2 teaspoons extra-virgin olive oil
2 to 4 tablespoons cold water

1. Preheat the oven to 325 degrees F.
2. In a mixing bowl, toss the garlic pieces with the olive oil to coat evenly. Spread the garlic pieces evenly on the bottom of a small baking pan and roast until their edges begin to brown, 25 to 30 minutes.
3. Remove the pan and with a spoon or spatula, scrape up and turn the garlic; then return the pan to the oven and roast until the garlic is uniformly golden brown, about 15 minutes more. Set aside to cool completely.
4. Put the roasted garlic pieces and 2 tablespoons of the water in a food processor fitted with the steel blade. Process, scraping the bowl down occasionally, until the garlic is pureed to a paste with the consistency of smooth peanut butter. If necessary, add the remaining water. Transfer to a bowl, cover and refrigerate until ready to use.

Yield: 1/2 cup

About California Pizza Kitchen:

California Pizza Kitchen® opened in 1985. All of their innovative pizzas are creatively designed and hearth-baked to perfection.

Carl's Jr. Famous Star

Description: *Duplicate your own version of this grilled burger with its secret sauce.*

Ingredients

1 sesame-seed hamburger bun	2 teaspoons mayonnaise
2 onion rings	3 dill pickle slices
1/2 teaspoon sweet pickle relish	chopped lettuce
1 1/2 teaspoon catsup	2 tomato slices
1/4 lb ground beef	
salt, to taste	

1. Preheat grill to high.
2. Using skillet, over medium heat, toast split bun, face down until lightly toasted; set aside.
3. Cut onion rings in quarters; set aside. In small bowl, combine ketchup and mustard (this is your special sauce); set aside.
4. Form beef into thin patty slightly larger than the bun; grill 2 to 3 minutes on each side or to desired doneness; season lightly with salt.
5. Divide mayonnaise and spread over heel and crown of bun.
6. Assemble sandwich: Top heel of bun with pickles, lettuce, tomato slices, onion, patty, special sauce, crown of bun. Serve.

Serves 1

About Carl's Jr:

Carl's Jr® debuted in 1956. It was modeled directly after the original McDonald's, which by then was pioneering the modern day fast food industry. Over the years Carl's Jr introduced several firsts to fast food restaurants like padded seating and partial dining room service.

Carrabba's Italian Grill Bruschette Carrabba

Description: *Garlic flavored bread topped with Italian cheeses, mushrooms and tomatoes.*

Ingredients

1 loaf Italian or French bread
1 stick butter, softened
3 - 4 cloves garlic, finely chopped
1/2 teaspoon garlic powder
3 slices Fontina cheese, thinly sliced and trimmed to fit bread slices
3 slices mozzarella cheese, thin-ly sliced and trimmed to fit bread slices
3 oz mushrooms, sliced, and sautéed in butter
3 slices Roma tomato, sliced ¼" thick
extra-virgin olive oil
pinch fresh basil, cut into fine strips (julienne strips)

1. Preheat oven to 450 degrees F.
2. Slice bread into ½-inch slices. Save ends for another recipe or for making bread crumbs.
3. In small bowl, combine softened butter with garlic and garlic powder; spread over bread slices. Top by layering with Fontina, mozzarella, mushrooms and tomatoes.
4. Bake in preheated oven for 4 to 5 minutes or until cheese has melted.
5. Remove from oven and drizzle with olive oil; sprinkle with fresh basil.

Serves 4

About Carrabbas Italian Grill:

Carrabbas Italian Grill® was founded in Houston by Johnny Carrabba and Damian Mandola in December of 1986. Many of the recipes on their menu are those of Damian's mother Grace and sister Rose. Damian preserved the Italian authenticity of Carrabba's food by traveling the world in search of unique Italian dishes and by taking numerous trips to his grandparents' native Italy.

The Cheesecake Factory Chicken Madeira

Description: *Sauteed chicken breast topped with fresh asparagus and melted mozzarella cheese, covered with fresh mushroom Madeira sauce. Serve with mashed potatoes*

Ingredients

1 tablespoon olive oil
4 boneless, skinless chicken
  breast fillets
8 asparagus spears
4 mozzarella cheese slices

Madeira Sauce:
2 tablespoons olive oil
2 cups sliced fresh mushrooms
3 cups Madeira wine
2 cups beef stock
1 tablespoon butter
1/4 teaspoon ground black
  pepper

1. Place chicken breasts between plastic wrap and pound to ¼-inch thickness; season with salt and pepper.
2. Heat oil in saute pan; add chicken and saute 4 to 6 minutes per side, until lightly browned; remove from pan and wrap in foil to keep warm.
3. Using the same pan, over medium heat, add 2 table-spoons oil and heat; add mushrooms and saute for 2 minutes. Add Madeira wine, stock, butter and pepper; bring to boil, reduce heat; simmer about 20 minutes or until sauce has reduced to ¼ of its original volume and is a dark brown color.
4. Meanwhile, bring a half saucepan of water to a boil; add salt; return to boil; add asparagus and boil 3 to 5 minutes. Immediately transfer to a bowl of ice water to stop the cooking process. The asparagus should be cooked crisp-tender.
5. Transfer cooked chicken to baking pan; top with mozzarella cheese and broil 3 to 4 minutes or until light brown spots begin to appear on the cheese.
6. To serve, arrange 2 breasts on each plate, top each with 4 asparagus spears, spoon 3 to 4 tablespoons of Madeira sauce over each.

Serves 4

The Cheesecake Factory "Mile-High" Meatloaf Sandwich

Description: *An open-faced meatloaf sandwich topped with mashed potatoes, crispy onion and BBQ gravy. Served on extra thick sliced egg bread.*

Ingredients

Meatloaf:
1 pound lean ground beef
1/2 pound ground pork
1/2 pound ground veal
3/4 cup large-curd cottage cheese
1/2 cup shredded Cheddar
1 cup chopped onions
1/2 cup chopped green pepper
1/2 cup dry, unseasoned bread crumbs
2 eggs
1/3 cup tomato sauce
1/4 cup dry red wine
1 tablespoon Dijon mustard
1 tablespoon salt or to taste
1/4 teaspoon pepper
1 loaf egg bread

Carmelized Onions:
2 tablespoons olive oil
2 tablespoons unsalted butter

4 cups thinly sliced onion
generous pinch of salt

Mushroom Sauce:
1 can brown gravy or homemade gravy
1/2 Vidalia onion finely diced
2 cloves garlic finely minced
1 portobello mushroom cap, finely chopped
1 tablespoon chopped parsley
1 tablespoon olive oil
1 tablespoon balsamic vinegar

Mashed Potatoes:
4 cups red potatoes, cut into cubes
2 tablespoons horseradish
1/2 cup butter, softened
1 teaspoon salt and to taste
1 cup gouda cheese, shredded

1. Preheat oven to 350 degrees F.
2. In large bowl, combine meatloaf ingredients, mixing until well combined. Pack into 9 X 5-inch loaf pan and bake in preheated oven for 50 minutes or until done. Depending on the height of the loaf pan, you

may want to place on a lipped baking-sheet to catch any juices that may overflow - not to mess your oven.

3. Meanwhile, melt butter and oil in a heavy saute pan. Brown onions slowly over medium heat for about a half hour; toward the end, add pinch of salt.

4. Prepare Mushroom Sauce: Saute onions, garlic, parsley and mushrooms in olive oil until onions are soft. Mix in brown gravy and balsamic vinegar; blend well; bring to boil; lower heat and simmer 5 minutes.

5. Prepare mashed potatoes: Place potato cubes in saucepan and cover with water; boil until soft; drain. Add butter, horseradish and salt; whip until smooth; beat in cheese until smooth; add more salt if needed.

6. To assemble sandwich: Cut egg bread in thick slices; top with meatloaf, onions, potatoes and cover with sauce.

Serves 4

RecipeSecrets.net tip:
You can substitute beef broth for the wine.

Chick-Fil-A Chicken Salad Sandwich

Description: *The perfect chicken salad with just enough creaminess, a hint of sweetness, a bit of crunch and served on wholegrain bread.*

Ingredients

2/3 - 1 cup mayonnaise
1/3 cup very finely diced celery
1/4 cup sweet pickle relish
2 tablespoons dried onion flakes
1 tablespoon buttermilk
1/2 teaspoon sugar
1/4 teaspoon salt

1/4 teaspoon freshly ground
 pepper
1/8 teaspoon garlic powder
2 cups cooked chicken meat, cut
 into small chunks
sliced whole grain bread

RecipeSecrets.net tip:
Substitute fresh minced
onion for the onion flakes.

1. In medium bowl, combine mayonnaise, celery, relish, onion flakes, buttermilk, sugar, salt, pepper and garlic powder; mix well.
2. Add chicken and toss to combine.
3. Use as a sandwich filling on whole grain bread.

Serves 4

About Chick-Fil-A:

In 1946 The Dwarf Grill opened and in 1964 they invented the original chicken sandwich. It's popularity brought about the opening of the first mall location of Chick-Fil-A® in 1967. In 1982 they were the first chain to sell chicken nuggets nationally. In 1986 they opened their first free-standing restaurant. They now have expanded their menu and they have over 1,000 locations.

Chick-Fil-A Coleslaw

Description: *This creamy, seeded slaw will go well with your favorite dishes.*

Ingredients

6 cups shredded cabbage
1/4 cup sugar
1 cup shredded carrots
1/2 teaspoon salt
1/4 teaspoon pepper
1/4-1/2 cup whole milk
1/2 cup mayonnaise (not Miracle
  Whip)
1/2 teaspoon celery seed

2-3 drops hot sauce
3 tablespoons dried minced
  onion
1/4-1/2 cup buttermilk

RecipeSecrets.net tip:
Make your own buttermilk by combining 1/2 cup milk and 2 teaspoons lemon juice. Let stand for 10 minutes.

1. In large bowl, combine all ingredients, mixing well.

2. Cover and refrigerate.

Serves 8

Chili's Asian Lettuce Wraps

Description: *Delicate lettuce cups filled with true Asian-flavored chicken and water chestnut filling dotted with sliced almonds.*

Ingredients

1 tablespoon oil
4 chicken breasts
3 green onions
1/4 cup minced water chestnuts
1/4 cup sliced almonds
4-6 lettuce leaves

Stir Fry Sauce:
1/4 cup water
1 teaspoon cornstarch
1/3 cup soy sauce
1/4 cup sugar
1/4 cup vinegar
1 tablespoon oil
2 teaspoons sesame seeds
1 teaspoon red pepper flakes
1 teaspoon chili oil
1/2 teaspoon minced ginger

Sesame Ginger Dipping Sauce:
1/4 cup water
3/4 teaspoon cornstarch

1/3 cup sugar
1/3 cup vinegar
1/4 cup soy sauce
1 teaspoon minced ginger
1 teaspoon oil
1/2 teaspoon sesame seeds
1/4 teaspoon minced garlic
1 dash red pepper flakes
1 dash parsley

Peanut Dipping Sauce:
1/2 cup peanut butter
1/3 cup water
2 tablespoons vinegar
1/2 teaspoon minced ginger
1/8 teaspoon crushed red
  pepper flakes
1/4 cup sugar
1/4 teaspoon minced garlic
1/2 teaspoon chili oil
1/2 teaspoon oil
1 tablespoon brown sugar

1. Prepare stir fry sauce: In a saucepan, combine water and cornstarch, stirring until cornstarch is dissolved. Add remaining ingredients. Place over medium heat; bring to boil; reduce heat; simmer to thicken.

2. Prepare the sesame ginger dipping sauce: In small saucepan, combine water and cornstarch; mix until cornstarch is dissolved. Add remaining ingredients; place over medium heat; bring to boil; reduce heat; simmer 2 minutes.

RecipeSecrets.net tip: Try substituting pork in this recipe.

3. Prepare peanut dipping sauce: In a small saucepan, combine all ingredients; whisk over low heat until smooth. Remove from heat when done.

4. Slice chicken breasts into strips. Heat oil in wok or large skillet over medium heat; add chicken; cook until done. Add water chestnuts; heat through. Add a bit more than ¼ cup stir-fry sauce; heat for 2 minutes; stir often. The sauce will bubble. Add onions; stir.

5. Shape lettuce leaves into "cups". Spoon chicken into cups and serve with dipping sauces on the side.

Serves 4

About Chili's:

When the first Chili's® restaurant opened in Dallas in 1975, the menu consisted of little more than burgers, chili, and tacos – yet there was a never-ending line out the door. Today, their permanent and limited-time menu items are even more exciting and innovative than ever.

Chili's Presidente Margarita

Description: *Just another fabulous margarita that you can duplicate at home.*

Ingredients

1 1/4 ounces Sauzas Commemorativo Tequila
1/2 ounce Presidente brandy
1/2 ounce Cointreau liqueur
4 ounces sour mix
splash of lime juice

1. Pour all ingredients into a shaker glass with crushed ice.
2. Shake very well and serve in a salt rimmed margarita glass with some ice.

Serves 1

Chipotle Mexican Grill Chicken & Marinade

Description: *Marinated chicken breasts with a nice kick.*

Ingredients

1 (2 ounce) package dried
  ancho chiles
1 teaspoon black pepper
2 teaspoons cumin powder
2 tablespoons fresh oregano,
  chopped

6 cloves garlic
1/2 red onion, quartered
1/4 cup vegetable oil
4 chicken breasts (6 ounces
  each)
salt, to taste

1. Place dry chilies in small bowl, cover with water, refrigerate overnight to soften.
2. Next day: Drain and discard water. Remove seeds from chilies and transfer to food processor.
3. Add remaining ingredients (except chicken) to processor and puree until smooth.
4. Spread mixture over chicken (or other meats that can be used), place in single layer on platter; cover; refrigerate at least one hour or up to 24 hours.
5. When ready to cook, preheat grill to 400 degrees F. If cooking indoors, heat a small amount of oil in heavy skillet over high heat. Salt meat to taste, grill lightly, turning only once. (Four minutes per side for chicken; 8 to 10 minutes per side for a ¾-inch thick steak). Serve hot.

Serves 4

About Chipotle Mexican Grill:

The first Chipotle Mexican Grill opened near the University of Denver in 1993. Their unique motto of "Food With Integrity" focuses on using ingredients that are unprocessed, family-farmed, sustainable, nutritious, naturally raised, added hormone free, organic, and artisanal.

Chipotle Honey Vinaigrette

Description: *A tangy and sweet dressing just perfect for your salads. Excellent with greens and also as a dressing for your favorite hoagie sandwiches.*

Ingredients

1/2 cup red wine vinegar
1/3 cup honey
2 teaspoons Grey Poupon Dijon mustard
1 1/4 teaspoons ground chipotle powder
1 teaspoon fresh lime juice
3/4 teaspoon black pepper
3/4 teaspoon salt

1/2 teaspoon paprika
1/4 teaspoon garlic powder
1/4 teaspoon onion powder
1/4 teaspoon dried oregano
1/2 cup extra virgin olive oil

1. Place all ingredients in blender (except oil); blend on low speed for 10 seconds.
2. Slowly drizzle olive oil into blender while running on low speed.
3. Transfer to covered container and refrigerate for at least an hour before using.

Yield: 1.5 cups

Church's Honey Biscuits with Honey Butter

Description: *Wholesome old-fashioned flaky biscuits sweetened with honey-butter brushed on the tops.*

Ingredients

2 cups all-purpose flour
4 teaspoons baking powder
1/2 teaspoon salt
2 teaspoons granulated sugar
1/2 cup vegetable shortening

1 teaspoon cream of tartar
2/3 cup whole milk
1/4 cup (1/2 stick) butter, melted
1/3 cup honey

1. Preheat oven to 450 degrees F.
2. In large bowl, combine flour, baking powder, sugar, salt, and cream of tartar. Cut in shortening using pastry blender or two forks until mixture resembles cornmeal.
3. Add milk; mix well. Turn onto floured surface and knead 12 to 15 minutes. Pull off portions of ¼ to 1/3-cup size. Gently roll and pat to ½-inch thickness.
4. Place on baking sheet and brush with melted butter.
5. Bake in preheated oven for 10 to 12 minutes or until golden.
6. Meanwhile make Honey Butter by adding honey to remaining melted butter. When biscuits are done, remove from oven and immediately brush with honey butter.

Makes one dozen

About Church's:

George W. Church, Sr., of San Antonio, Texas, founded Church's in 1952, at a time when only hot dogs and ice cream were being marketed as fast food. The first Church's Fried Chicken To Go, in downtown San Antonio across the street from the Alamo, sold only fried chicken. French fries and jalapeño peppers were added to the menu by 1955.

Claim Jumper Chocolate Motherlode Cake & Frosting

Description: *Chocolate cake with chocolate chips and chocolate fudge frosting.*

Ingredients

6 eggs
3 cups sugar
6 tablespoons butter, softened
3 cups vegetable oil
1 1/2 cups unsweetened cocoa
  powder
1 1/2 cups buttermilk
3 teaspoons vanilla extract
6 3/4 cups flour
4 1/2 teaspoons baking powder
4 1/2 teaspoons baking soda
3/4 teaspoon salt
3 cups boiling water
3 cups chocolate chips

Chocolate Motherlode Frosting:
1 lb fine-quality semisweet
  chocolate
1 cup heavy cream
2 tablespoons sugar
2 tablespoons light corn syrup
1/4 cup unsalted butter, cut into
  pieces

1. Preheat oven to 350 degrees F.
2. Grease and flour six 8-inch round cake pans; place ½ cup chocolate chips in each cake pan, spreading evenly; set aside.
3. In large bowl, combine eggs, sugar, butter, oil, cocoa powder, buttermilk and vanilla; blend well.
4. On waxed paper, sift together flour, baking powder, soda and salt; add to wet ingredients in the bowl, mixing well after each addition. Mix in boiling water.
5. Divide batter evenly between prepared pans.
6. Bake in oven for 25 minutes or until cake tests done. Cool 10 minutes in pan on wire racks before removing.
7. When completely cool, fill layers and ice with Chocolate Motherlode Frosting.
8. To prepare the frosting, chop the chocolate finely and

set aside.

9. Place cream, sugar and corn syrup in 1 ½ - 2-quart heavy saucepan. Bring to a boil over moderately low heat, whisking until the sugar is dissolved. Remove pan from heat and add chocolate continuing to whisk until the chocolate has melted. Add butter and continue to whisk until butter has melted.

10. Transfer frosting to a bowl and allow to cool, stirring occasionally. This mixture may have to be refrigerated to get it to a spreadable consistency depending on the type of chocolate used.

11. Fill and frost cake.

Makes 1 cake.

About Claim Jumper:

Claim Jumper® is famous for their large portions of comfort foods. First opened in 1977, and has close to 50 restaurants to date. Their extensive menu is popular with everyone - from children to seniors.

Claim Jumper Widow-Maker Burger

Description: *One very tall sandwich made from a double-thick burger topped with Cheddar, bacon, onion, lettuce, tomato and avocado with a mayo/relish dressing.*

Ingredients

8 ounce cooked hamburger patty
1 hamburger bun
2 slices bacon, cooked crisp
1 onion ring
1 ounce mayonnaise
2 ounces lettuce, shredded
2 ounces red relish (sweet or dill green may be used)
1/2 avocado, sliced

2 thin slices tomatoes
2 slices Cheddar cheese
salt and pepper

RecipeSecrets.net tip: When frying bacon, save your bacon grease. Strain through a cheese cloth. Cover and refrigerate and you will have bacon grease for sauting veggies and frying other foods.

1. Grill burger to desired doneness.
2. Meanwhile, in skillet, fry bacon until crisp; drain well.
3. Toast hamburger bun and spread with mayonnaise.
4. Build burger from the bottom heel: lettuce, onion ring, burger patty, bacon, relish, avocado, tomato and cheese. Top with crown. Serve hot.

Serves 1

Cracker Barrel Ham & Egg Casserole

Description: *A perfect breakfast or brunch casserole of eggs, ham and cheese.*

Ingredients

sourdough bread
4 to 5 eggs, beaten
1/4 cup evaporated milk
1/4 teaspoon salt
1/4 teaspoon pepper
1/3 cup diced cooked smoked ham
1/2 cup shredded mild Cheddar cheese

RecipeSecrets.net tip:
Sliced brown and serve
sausages can be used in
place of ham.

1. Spray casserole dish with non-stick cooking spray.

2. Slice bread and trim crusts from slices; place a layer of bread on the bottom of prepared casserole dish.

3. In medium bowl, beat eggs, evaporated milk, salt and pepper; mix well. Pour over bread slices; sprinkle with diced ham; cover and refrigerate over night or for at least 5 to 6 hours.

4. When ready to make, preheat oven to 375 degrees F. Remove casserole from refrigerator, uncover and sprinkle cheese over egg/ham mixture. Bake in preheated oven for 20 to 24 minutes depending on the size and depth of the casserole dish.

Serves 2

About Cracker Barrel:

Cracker Barrel® opened in 1969, serving good ol' country cookin' to their customers. Their cornbread comes from cornmeal, not a mix; mashed potatoes are made from real potatoes; and scratch biscuits come with real butter.

Cracker Barrel Lemon Ice Box Pie

Description: *A sweet, creamy and smooth lemony-flavored pie.*

Ingredients

1 9-inch graham cracker crust
1 can (14 oz.) sweetened condensed milk
3 egg yolks
3 ounces pure lemon juice
4 ounces Cool Whip, thawed
14 vanilla wafers

RecipeSecrets.net tip:
You can use your own homemade baked crust for this recipe.

1. In medium bowl, combine milk, yolks and lemon juice using wire whisk.

2. Transfer to pie shell; arrange vanilla wafers around pie, pushing into the filling so only ½ the wafer is showing.

3. Spread cool whip evenly over top; cover with plastic wrap.

4. Place in freezer; freeze at least 2 hours. Best served very cold.

Makes 1 pie.

Cracker Barrel Pinto Beans

Description: *An healthy side dish to compliment your entrée made the old-fashioned way.*

Ingredients

1 pound ham hocks
1 tablespoon sugar
water, enough to cover ham hocks
2 cups dry pinto beans
8 cups water
1 1/2 teaspoon salt

RecipeSecrets.net tip:
Ham hocks are usually used to flavor soups, stews, and bean dishes that require longer cooking.

1. Place ham hocks and sugar in saucepan and cover with water. Bring to simmer; simmer until done and ham hocks are tender.

2. When done, remove from broth but do not discard broth. Using two forks, separate meat from fat, skin and bones. Return meat to broth; cool and store in freezer until bean day. (Great make-ahead meal).

3. When preparing beans, sort and pick through beans; wash; transfer to large pot with 8 cups water, salt, ham and ham broth; bring to boil, cover and simmer about 3 hours or until beans are tender.

Serves 6

Cracker Barrel Sweet Potato Casserole

Description: *Sweet and citrusy potatoes with a pecan topping.*

Ingredients

5 1/2 lbs sweet potatoes,
  boiled tender, skinned
8 ounces margarine
1/4 cup orange juice
  concentrate (thawed, not
  diluted)
8 ounces brown sugar, firmly
  packed
1 tablespoon grated orange rind

Topping:
2 ounces margarine
7 ounces brown sugar, firmly
  packed
2 ounces milk
4 ounces pecan pieces

RecipeSecrets.net tip:
Potatoes can be cooked
ahead of time, cooled, covered and refrigerated.

1. Preheat oven to 400 degrees F. Butter casserole dish and set aside.

2. While potatoes are cooking, prepare the topping: Combine all topping ingredients in saucepan and bring to a boil, stirring constantly, until thickened.

3. Place potatoes, margarine, brown sugar, orange juice concentrate and orange rind in large bowl; blend well; transfer to prepared casserole. Pour prepared topping over potatoes and bake in preheated oven for 20 to 30 minutes.

Serves 8.

Dave and Buster's Cheeseburger Pizza

Description: *A cheeseburger made into a pizza.*

Ingredients

1 tablespoon cornmeal
8 to 10 ounces pizza dough
2 tablespoons olive oil
3 tablespoons ketchup/mustard
mix (50/50 mix of ketchup and
mustard)
3/4 cup American cheese,
shredded
1 cup char-grilled burger
2 tablespoons kosher pickle
slices (julienned)
2 tablespoons sliced red onions

1/2 cup mozzarella cheese,
shredded

Garnish:
1 tablespoon spicy ketchup
1 tablespoon real crispy bacon
bits
2 slices tomatoes
1/2 cup shredded lettuce
2 tablespoons diced onions

RecipeSecrets.net tip:
Use a blend of white and
yellow American cheese in
this recipe.

1. Preheat oven to 450 degrees F.
2. Lightly sprinkle cornmeal on pizza tin; set aside.
3. Roll dough into a 10 - 12 inch circle on a floured surface; transfer to prepared pizza tin.
4. Spread with ketchup/mustard mixture almost to edges of dough.
5. Top with cheese mixture - almost to edges of dough.
6. Top with diced burger, pickles, red onions and mozzarella.
7. Bake in preheated oven 12 to 15 minutes or until crust is golden and cheese is melted.
8. Remove from oven and top with spicy ketchup, bacon bits, shredded lettuce, tomato slices and diced onions.

9. Season with salt, pepper, garlic and parsley. Add
   seasoned salt if desired.

Serves 2

About Dave & Buster's:

In the late 70's in Little Rock, Arkansas, there were
two businesses next door to each other. A man
named Buster ran a casual restaurant and a man
named Dave ran "Slick Willy's World of
Entertainment."

The two men eventually became friends and noticed
that patrons would be seen going from one business
to the other. That inspired them to combine their
businesses and create Dave and Busters - a fun
place to eat, play games, and have a good time.

Denny's Bacon Caesar Burger

Description: *A tasty burger served with Caesar dressing on the side for dipping.*

Ingredients

1 hamburger bun
1 hamburger patty
1 leaf Romaine lettuce
2 hamburger dill slices
1 slice red onion
2 tomato slices
2 slices Monterey Jack cheese
2 slices bacon cooked
1/4 cup Caesar dressing, served on the side

RecipeSecrets.net tip:
Your burger can be skillet fried, broiled or grilled to desired doneness.

1. On griddle or in heavy skillet, cook patty, seasoning to taste with salt and pepper.
2. Toast bun separately.
3. Assemble sandwich by starting with the heel of the bun; layer with romaine, tomato slices, pickle slices, onion slice, patty, cheese and bacon; place crown on top.
4. Serve immediately with dressing on the side.

Serves 1

About Denny's:

The restaurant chain that we know as Denny's® began in Lakewood, Calif. in 1953 with a dream and a donut stand called Danny's Donuts. In 1959, Danny's was renamed Denny's to avoid confusion with another small chain in Southern California called "Coffee Dan's." Doughnuts were phased out and the menu grew to include sandwiches and other entrees.

El Torito's Mexican Caesar Salad

Description: *Strips of crisp-fried tortillas on top of a bed of greens with roasted red pepper strips drizzled with a creamy and zesty dressing with a kick.*

Ingredients

Cilantro Pepita Dressing:
2 medium Anaheim chiles, roasted, peeled and seeded
1/3 cup roasted pepitas (pumpkin seeds)
2 garlic cloves, peeled
1/4 teaspoon ground black pepper
1 teaspoon salt
12 ounces salad oil
1/4 cup red wine vinegar
5 tablespoons grated Cotija cheese (see note)
2 small bunches cilantro, stemmed

1 1/2 cup mayonnaise
1/4 cup water

Salad:
2 corn tortillas
vegetable oil
1 large head romaine lettuce, rinsed and spun dry
1/3 cup finely grated Cotija cheese
roasted red bell pepper, peeled and cut into julienne strips
1/2 cup pepitas (roasted pumpkin seeds)

RecipeSecrets.net tip: Cotija cheese is a hard cheese, similar to Parmesan.

1. Place chilies, pepitas, garlic, pepper, salt, oil, vinegar, and cheese in bowl of food processor and blend approximately 10 seconds; add cilantro, a little at a time until blended smooth. This may have to be done in batches.

2. In large stainless steel bowl, combine mayonnaise and water; whisk until smooth. Transfer chili mixture to bowl; whisk to blend thoroughly.

3. Transfer to covered container and refrigerate. Will keep for three days.

4. Assemble salad by cutting corn tortillas into match-stick size strips. Heat oil in saute pan; fry tortilla strips until crisp; remove with slotted spoon; drain on paper towels; set aside.
5. Tear romaine into bite-sized pieces; place on salad plates; ladle about 2 ounces of dressing over each salad.
6. Top with cheese and tortilla strips. Arrange four red pepper strips (like spokes of a wheel) on top of each salad; garnish with whole pepitas.

Serves 4

About El Torito's:

El Torito's® Sports Bar opened in 1982 serving flavorful, succulent, meaty pork ribs, peel-your-own shrimp and tangy BBQ chicken as well as many other favorites.

Emeril's Southwest Seasoning

Description: *A great seasoning for just about anything. Flavor your beef, chicken, fish - get creative.*

Ingredients

2 tablespoons chili powder
2 teaspoons ground cumin
2 tablespoons paprika
1 teaspoon black pepper
1 tablespoon ground coriander
1 teaspoon cayenne pepper
1 tablespoon garlic powder
1 teaspoon crushed red pepper
1 tablespoon salt

1 tablespoon dried oregano

1. Combine all ingredients thoroughly.
2. Store in air-tight container.

About Emeril:

Emeril Lagasse® is popularly known for his cooking show and enthusiastic slogan "BAM." He is the star of the Food Network and owner of many successful restaurants.

Famous Dave's Sloppy Ques

Description: *Sloppy joes done only the way Famous Dave can. Well-seasoned with a bit of heat.*

Ingredients

1 pound ground beef
1/2 cup finely chopped sweet
  yellow onion
1/4 cup finely chopped green
  bell pepper
1 jalapeno, finely minced
1 teaspoon steak & burger
  seasoning mix

1 tablespoon chili powder
1/4 teaspoon cayenne
1 1/2 cups BBQ sauce
1 teaspoon prepared mustard
4 hamburger buns, split,
  buttered, toasted

RecipeSecrets.net tip: McCormick® Spicy Montreal Steak Seasoning works great in this recipe.

1. In heavy skillet, over medium-high heat, brown ground beef; drain well. Add onion, green pepper, jalapeno, seasoning and chili powder. Stir well to combine and crumble; continue cooking until beef is thoroughly cooked, stirring constantly.

2. Add cayenne, BBQ sauce and mustard; stir well to combine and heat through.

3. Spoon onto split buns. Serve hot.

Makes 4 servings

About Famous Dave's:

Dave Anderson, founder of Famous Dave's opened his first restaurant in Wisconsin in 1994. Dave is a BBQ legend known for having smoked tons of ribs in an old garbage can. He perfected his system to smoke good "que" by first hand rubbing each slab with a blend of southern spices, then slow smoking 'em in a pit of smoldering hickory.

Girl Scout Thin Mint Cookies

Description: *Thin, crisp chocolate cookies covered in a smooth chocolate-mint coating.*

Ingredients

Chocolate Cookie Wafers:
1 18 ounce package chocolate
  fudge cake mix
3 tablespoons shortening,
  softened
1/2 cup cake flour, measured
  then sifted
1 egg
3 tablespoons water
non-stick cooking spray

Chocolate Coating:
3 12-ounce bags semi-sweet
  chocolate chips
3/4 teaspoon peppermint
  extract
6 tablespoons shortening

1. Begin by making the dough for the cookie wafers: Place cake mix, shortening, egg, water, oil and cocoa in large bowl; blend well. Cover and refrigerate 2 hours for easier handling.

2. When ready to make cookies: Preheat oven to 350 degrees F. spray cookie sheets with non-stick spray; set aside.

3. There are 2 ways these can be made. The first way is to roll a portion of the dough on a lightly floured surface to a thickness of 1/16-inch; cut with 1 ½-inch round cutter and place on baking sheet. The second way is to pinch off small ½-inch portions and shape into a ball. Place 2 inches apart on prepared baking sheet. Spray the flat and smooth bottom of a glass and press firmly on each shaped piece of dough to flatten.

4. Bake 8 to 10 minutes; remove to wire racks and allow to cool completely.

5. Prepare chocolate coating: In microwaveable-safe bowl combine chocolate chips, peppermint extract

and shortening; heat for 2 minutes on LOW; stir; heat another minute or until smooth; stir. This can also be done in the top of a double boiler over simmering water.

6. Dip each wafer in chocolate; allow excess to drip off. Place on waxed paper lined baking sheet and refrigerate until firm.

Serves 8

About Girl Scouts:

The Girl Scouts® are famous for their delicious cookies. No longer made by the Girl Scouts, the cookies have been made by ABC Bakers since 1939.

Golden Corral Banana Pudding

Description: *A rich, sweet blend of condensed milk, pudding and Cool Whip layered between banana slices and vanilla wafers.*

Ingredients

1 (14 oz) can sweetened condensed milk
1 1/2 cup cold water (or milk)
1 (4 oz) size package instant vanilla pudding
2 cups Cool Whip
1 box vanilla wafers
3 bananas, sliced

1. In large bowl, mix sweetened condensed milk with water; add pudding mix; beat well. Chill in refrigerator for 5 minutes.

2. Fold in thawed Cool Whip.

3. Spoon 1 cup of pudding in bottom of serving dish; top with 1/3 of the bananas, 1/3 of the wafers and 1/3 of the pudding. Repeat layering twice, ending with pudding. Top with vanilla wafers. Chill thoroughly; keep refrigerated.

RecipeSecrets.net tip:
For an more intense banana flavor, use instant banana-flavored pudding.

Serves 6

About Golden Corral:

Golden Corral® is a family-style restaurant chain that features a large buffet and grill offering numerous hot and cold item, a carving station and their Brass Bell Bakery.

Hard Rock Cafe Handmade Onion Rings

Description: *Golden fried onion rings seasoned with Hard Rock Cafe's own seasoning.*

Ingredients

1 yellow onion, sliced into ½-inch rings, save inner rings for another recipe, soak the larger rings in cold water
flour to coat
3 eggs blended with 1/2 cup milk (egg wash)
bread crumbs to coat
vegetable oil for deep frying

1/2 cup kosher salt
1 1/2 teaspoons onion powder
1 1/2 teaspoons garlic powder
1 1/2 teaspoons coarse black pepper
1 1/2 teaspoons celery salt

1. Place flour in shallow dish.
2. Place breadcrumbs in separate shallow dish.
3. In another shallow dish, combine eggs and milk; mix well.
4. Remove onion rings from water; shake off excess water; place in flour and coat evenly.
5. Place floured onions (shake off excess flour) in egg wash; coat well; shake off excess flour and place onions in breadcrumbs; coat well. Shake off excess breadcrumbs.
6. Heat oil to 350 degrees F. Place onion rings in a fry basket, fry 3 minutes or until golden brown and fully cooked. Remove from oil; drain well.
7. While onions are frying, in a small container, combine kosher salt, onion powder, garlic powder, coarse black pepper and celery salt. Mix thoroughly. Sprinkle salt mixture (called Hard Rock Cafe seasoning) over hot onion rings. Serve immediately.

Serves 4

About Hard Rock Cafe:

Hard Rock Cafe® is known throughout the world - owning the world's greatest collection of music memorabilia which they display in all their locations. The first Hard Rock Cafe opened its doors to the public in 1971 in London, England.

Hard Rock Cafe Pig Sandwich

Description: *A tasty pulled pork sandwich smothered in slaw and a zesty BBQ sauce.*

Ingredients

8 Hamburger buns

Pulled Pork:
1 quart hot water
1 quart apple cider vinegar
1/2 cup Tabasco sauce
1/2 cup sugar
3 lbs. pork shoulder, boned

Pig Slaw:
1/4 cup sugar
3 cups white vinegar
2 1/4 cups water
1 head green cabbage leaf, peeled and cored

Pig Sauce:
2 cups Heinz ketchup
2 1/4 cups cider vinegar
1 3/4 teaspoons salt
1/2 cup sugar
1 1/2 tablespoons Worcestershire sauce
1 1/2 tablespoons coarse black pepper
1 1/2 tablespoons chili powder
1/2 teaspoon garlic salt
1/2 teaspoon granulated garlic
3 tablespoons vegetable oil

RecipeSecrets.net tip: Pork can be cooked in your slow cooker for 6 to 8 hours on low.

1. Prepare pulled pork: In large bowl, dissolve sugar in hot water; add vinegar and Tabasco; mix well. Place pork in marinade making sure marinade covers pork; cover; refrigerate for at least 12 hours. Turn occasionally.

2. To cook pork: Preheat oven to 450 degrees F. Transfer pork to baking dish; bake until well-browned. Reduce heat to 300 degrees F. and pour some of the marinade over the roast. Cover with foil and slowroast for an additional 2 hours or until meat pulls away from bone easily. Discard remaining marinade.

3. Prepare pig slaw: In large bowl, dissolve sugar in vinegar; add water; whisk well; add cabbage; mix well; cover; refrigerate.

4. Prepare pig sauce: In medium saucepan, combine all ingredients (except oil); mix well and bring to boil. Add oil; stir to blend. Lower heat and simmer for 20 minutes to thicken. Continue to stir. Cool completely; cover; store in refrigerator until ready to use. When ready to serve: Toast hamburger buns. Place a scoop of pulled pork on the heel of the bun; top with pig slaw; ladle pig sauce over slaw and meat. Top with crown. Serve with onion rings, dill pickle slices and a side of slaw.

Serves 8

Hard Rock Cafe Twisted Mac and Cheese

Description: *A rich mac and cheese dish using Cheddar and Monterey Jack cheeses and sprinkled with Parmesan breadcrumbs.*

Ingredients

2 cups cavatappi pasta (any pasta works)
1/3 cup whole milk
4 oz Velveeta cheese spread
1/2 cup shredded Cheddar
1/2 cup shredded Monterey jack
1/8 teaspoon ground cayenne pepper
1/8 teaspoon ground black pepper

1/4 cup diced roasted red bell pepper
2 teaspoon Italian seasoned bread crumbs
2 teaspoon grated Parmesan
1/4 teaspoon finely minced parsley

1. In large saucepan, bring water to a boil and cook pasta according to directions on package; drain; do not rinse.
2. Using same saucepan, combine Velveeta, Cheddar, Jack cheese, cayenne pepper and black pepper; heat over low heat about 10 minutes, stirring, until cheeses have melted and sauce is smooth.
3. Return pasta to pan; add roasted pepper; toss to coat.
4. In small bowl, combine breadcrumbs, Parmesan and parsley; mix well.
5. Transfer hot pasta to serving dish; sprinkle with breadcrumb mixture. Serve immediately.

Serves 4

Hardee's Peach Cobbler

Description: *Easy to make treat with peaches and a touch of cinnamon and sugar.*

Ingredients

1 large can peach pie filling
1 frozen pie crust, thawed
1/4 cup (1/2 stick) butter, cut into pats - thin slices
cinnamon
sugar

1. Preheat oven to 375 degrees F.
2. Spread pie filling evenly in bottom of square baking pan; top with slices of butter - evenly spaced.
3. Carefully remove pie crust from the pan it is in and carefully place over filling in pan. Cut edges that hang over to make fit on the square pan. Not to waste the remaining crust, you can use little cookie cutters and place over top of pie for decoration.
4. Sprinkle generously with cinnamon and sugar; bake in preheated oven for 20 to 25 minutes or until crust is lightly browned.
5. Serve with a scoop of vanilla ice cream.

Serves 4

About Hardee's:

The first Hardee's® hamburger stand opened in 1960. The concept was simple, charcoal-broiled hamburgers and milkshakes sold for 15 cents each.

Houlihan's Jambalaya Rice

Description: *Sausage, peppers, onions and chicken with tomatoes in a chicken base seasoned with that kick we all love.*

Ingredients

1 1/2 tablespoons vegetable oil
1 cup andouille sausage, diced
  large
1 cup yellow onion, diced
1/2 cup green pepper, diced
1/2 cup celery
1 cup chicken diced
1/2 teaspoon salt
1/4 teaspoon cayenne pepper

1/2 teaspoon white pepper
1 teaspoon black pepper
1/4 teaspoon thyme
1/4 tablespoon Tabasco
1/4 cup garlic, pureed
2 tablespoon chicken base
1/2 cup canned diced tomatoes,
  drained well
2 cups white rice

1. Preheat oven to 350 degrees F.
2. In large skillet, add oil and heat. Add sausage; saute until crisp; add vegetables; saute until tender; mix well.
3. Add chicken; saute another 2 minutes.
4. Add seasonings, garlic puree and chicken base; cook approximately 3 to 5 minutes. Add tomatoes; mix well; cook an additional 4 minutes.
5. Stir in rice; cook 2 minutes.
6. Transfer to large baking dish and cover with foil. Place in preheated oven and bake for 20 to 30 minutes or until rice is tender. Serve hot.

Serves 4

About Houlihan's:

Houlihan's® first opened their doors in 1972, in Kansas City. At Houlihan's they make everything the hard way - from scratch. From appetizers and salads to entrees and desserts, it's all prepared fresh daily.

Houlihan's 'Shrooms

Description: *Cheese filled mushroom caps breaded and deep fried until golden brown.*

Ingredients

6 large button mushrooms
1 cup bleached flour
1 1/2 teaspoons salt
1/2 teaspoon cayenne pepper
1/2 cup buttermilk
vegetable oil for frying

Cheese Filling:
1/3 cup whipped cream cheese
1/4 cup shredded sharp Cheddar
cheese
1/2 teaspoon dry Hidden Valley
Ranch Dressing Mix

1. Prepare cheese filling: In small bowl, combine cream cheese, Cheddar and dressing mix; blend well; let stand 10 minutes.
2. While filling is resting, clean mushrooms and remove stems.
3. Fill mushroom caps with filling.
4. In small bowl, combine flour, 1 ½ teaspoons salt and cayenne pepper.
5. In separate small bowl, pour in milk.
6. Dip filled mushroom into milk, shake off excess and then dip in flour mixture, shake off excess flour; repeat process, place coated mushrooms on baking sheet and place in freezer; freeze for at least 3 hours.
7. When frozen, heat oil in deep fryer to 350 degrees F. Fry 8 to 10 minutes or until golden; drain on paper towels. Serve hot.

Serves 4

Ikea Swedish Meatballs

Description: *Nicely seasoned beef and pork meatballs served with a gravy-cream sauce.*

Ingredients

1 small onion, finely chopped
1 tablespoon vegetable oil
2/3 pound lean ground beef
1/3 pound ground lean pork
1/2 cup bread crumbs
1 cup milk
1 egg, lightly beaten
1 teaspoon salt
1 teaspoon black pepper

1/4 teaspoon ground allspice
1 tablespoon vegetable oil (for frying)
1 (10 ounce) can beef gravy
1/2 cup cream

1. In saute pan, heat 1 tablespoon oil and add onions; saute until soft and clear; set aside.
2. In small bowl, combine breadcrumbs with milk, let soak for 10 minutes.
3. In large bowl, combine onions, breadcrumb/milk mixture, egg, meat and seasonings; mix well. Form into small meatballs.
4. Place meatballs in large hot skillet, with 1 tablespoon oil. Brown meatballs; cook until cooked through.
5. In small saucepan, combine gravy and cream; heat through but do not boil.
6. Serve meatballs with gravy and boiled potatoes or hot cooked pasta.

Serves 4-6

Jack In The Box Oreo Cookie Shake

Description: *This is bound to become a favorite with any Oreo lover.*

Ingredients

3 cups vanilla ice cream
1 1/2 cups milk
8 Oreo cookies

1. Combine the ice cream and milk in a blender and mix on low speed until smooth.
2. Break Oreo cookies into pieces while adding them to the blender. Mix on low speed for 5 to 10 seconds or until the cookies are mostly pureed into the shake, but a few larger pieces remain. Use a spoon to break up any larger chunks.
3. Pour shake into two glasses.

Serves 2

About Jack In The Box:

Robert Peterson started the original Jack in the Box® in 1951 with a drive-thru restaurant in San Diego. Before 1980, Jack's mascot clown's existence was that as a fixture on the drive-thru speaker. The company decided an image change towards more "adult fare" was in order, and in a commercial, they blew up the drive-thru clown.

The Jack in the Box menu is extensive. There's the usual line of burgers and an interesting line of alternates like egg rolls, bacon potato cheddar wedges, and tacos.

Jiffy Corn Muffin Mix

Description: *Save money and time and always have this mix on hand for use in many dishes as well as for cornbreads and corn muffins.*

Ingredients

2/3 cup all purpose flour
1/2 cup yellow corn meal
3 tablespoons granulated sugar
1 tablespoon baking powder
1/4 teaspoon salt
2 tablespoons vegetable oil

To Prepare Corn Muffins:
1 egg
1/3 cup milk

1. Combine flour, corn meal, sugar, baking powder and salt. Mix well with wire whisk.
2. Whisk in vegetable oil and mix until dry mixture is smooth and lumps are gone.

If you wish to make Corn Muffins:

1. Preheat oven to 400 degrees F. Combine above mixture with egg and milk. Mix well.
2. Fill muffin tins 1/2 full. Bake 15-20 minutes.

Makes 6 muffins.

About Jiffy:

Jiffy® mix brand was introduced in 1930. These little boxes of various mixes are perfect for the busy cook.

Jimmy Buffett's Margaritaville Restaurant Jalapeno Macaroni & Cheese

Description: *A new twist on mac and cheese for those that like the heat. Jalapeno peppers give this dish that extra kick.*

Ingredients

8 tablespoons butter, melted
1/2 pound cream cheese, melted
2 1/2 cups heavy cream
1 teaspoon salt
1/4 teaspoon Tony Chachere's
Seasoning *(see page 154)*
1/2 pound Cheddar cheese

1/3 cup flour
1 cup sliced jalapenos
1/2 cup jalapeno juice (from jar)
2 tablespoons bread crumbs
1 pound Perciatel - 10-inch
macaroni noodles

1. In saucepan, melt butter; add cream cheese; mix until well blended; add heavy cream; whisk well to combine. Whisk in jalapeno juice; mix well.

2. Add Cheddar, stirring until Cheddar is completely melted. Add sliced jalapeno, salt, Tony C's and flour; continue whisking until thoroughly blended.

3. Spray loaf pan with non-stick spray; preheat oven to 350 degrees F.

4. Spoon a layer of cooked macaroni in prepared loaf pan; top with cheese sauce; add another layer of macaroni; top with cheese sauce. Top with bread crumbs, cover, and place in preheated oven. Bake 30 minutes; uncover and bake and additional 20 to 30 minutes or until light brown.

Serves 8

About Jimmy Buffett's Margaritaville Restaurant:

Margaritaville® is an experience unlike any other... It's not just a dining destination, it's an entire change of latitude. Whether it's the Jumbies on stilts, the volcanos erupting with margaritas, the pool side that wraps around the bar, or the frozen concoctions, a trip to Margaritaville will not soon be forgotten.

Joe's Crab Shack Crab Dip

Description: *A wonderful combination of crab meat, onions and peppers combined with cream cheese and sour cream - infused with just the right seasoning.*

Ingredients

2 oz cream cheese, softened
4 teaspoons diced yellow onion
1 tablespoon butter, softened
4 teaspoons finely diced green
  pepper
1/2 cup sour cream
1/4 teaspoon seasoned salt
1/8 teaspoon paprika

1 tablespoon mayonnaise
1/4 cup shredded Mozzarella
  cheese
1 (6 oz.) can crab meat, drained
fresh diced green onion, for
  garnish
fresh chopped parsley, for
  garnish

1. Preheat oven to 350 degrees F. Lightly grease a small, shallow baking dish; set aside.

2. In small bowl, combine cream cheese, mayonnaise, sour cream and butter; beat until smooth; add seasoned salt and paprika; stir well.

RecipeSecrets.net tip: For the best flavor, use fresh crab meat.

3. Add onions, crab meat, green pepper and mozzarella; blend.

4. Transfer to prepared baking dish; bake in preheated oven 10 to 14 minutes to heat through.

5. Garnish with green onion and parsley. Serve with unsalted or lightly salted corn chips.

Serves 2-3 as an appetizer

About Joe's Crab Shack:

Specializing in crab dishes and delightful seafood, Joe's Crab Shack® is a fun place to be. The look of a shanty by the seaside helps create a casual environment which typically is popular with patrons and brimming with energy.

Joe's Crab Shack Popcorn Shrimp

Description: *Creole seasoning and a splash of Tabasco give these delicately golden fried shrimp their wonderful flavor.*

Ingredients

1 lb small fresh shrimp (cleaned and shelled)
4 tablespoons corn starch
2 eggs beaten
1/4 cup water
1 cup cracker meal
1 teaspoon garlic powder
1 teaspoon Creole seasoning

1 teaspoon brown sugar
1/3 cup plain bread crumbs
1/3 cup flour
1 1/2 teaspoon Tabasco sauce
1/2 teaspoon paprika

RecipeSecrets.net tip:
Serve with tartar sauce.

1. In medium bowl, combine shrimp, garlic powder, brown sugar and Tabasco sauce; mix well. Cover and refrigerate for 30 minutes to marinate.

2. In small bowl, beat egg and water; set aside.

3. In separate bowl, combine flour, cracker meal, bread crumbs, paprika and Creole seasoning; blend well.

4. Place cornstarch in separate bowl.

5. Heat oil for frying.

6. Working with one at a time, dust shrimp with cornstarch; place in egg wash; shake off excess; roll in cracker mixture. Place on plate until all are coated.

7. Fry in hot oil until golden brown. Shrimp will float to top when cooked through; remove from hot oil and place on paper towels to drain.

Serves 6

Kenny Rogers Koo Koo Roo Original Skinless Flame-Broiled Chicken

Description: *Skinless chicken pieces in a citrus-based marinade grilled with a mild BBQ baste.*

Ingredients

1 whole chicken, skinned and
cut into 8 pieces

Marinade:
1 cup water
1 cup apple juice
1 cup V-8 juice
1 tbsp lemon juice
1/2 cup pineapple juice
1 cup chopped onion
2 teaspoons salt
2 teaspoons ground black
pepper

Baste:
2 tablespoons plus 1 teaspoon
vegetable oil
1/2 cup thinly sliced onions
1 can (10 oz) tomato puree
1/4 cup water
1 tablespoon white vinegar
1 tablespoon lemon juice
1/4 teaspoon salt
dash ground black pepper
dash garlic powder

1. In non-reactive bowl, combine marinade ingredients.
2. Add chicken to marinade, turn to coat, cover and refrigerate at least 24 hours or up to 72 hours. Turn chicken pieces occasionally.
3. Prepare baste: In skillet, heat 1 teaspoon oil; add onions and saute until they begin to blacken a bit; transfer to medium saucepan and add remaining baste ingredients. Bring mixture to a full boil; reduce heat; simmer 5 to 7 minutes. Remove from heat and cool; cover and refrigerate until ready to use.
4. When ready to cook, remove chicken from marinade; discard marinade.
5. Grill chicken until just about done; brush with baste and continue to grill for several minutes; turn and baste other side and continue to grill until cooked

through.

Serves 6-8

About Kenny Rogers Roasters:

Kenny Rogers Roasters® opened in 1991 serving foods you would make at home like roasted chickens.

KFC Corn On The Cob

Description: *Another favorite from the Colonel - a flavor-enhanced ear of corn as a side dish.*

Ingredients

4-8 ears of fresh or frozen corn on the cob
1/2 teaspoon salt
1/2 teaspoon sugar
1/4 teaspoon ground black pepper
1/4 teaspoon Accent Flavor Enhancer
melted butter
milk

RecipeSecrets.net tip:
Accent is a flavor enhancer sold in the spice section of most supermarkets.

1. Cook corn in hot water with sugar and a splash of milk until the corn is tender.
2. Remove dip in melted butter that has been seasoned with salt, pepper and Accent.

Serves 4-8

About KFC:

KFC, also known as Kentucky Fried Chicken - opened in 1930 by Harlan Sanders as "Sander's Court & Café". In 1939 he begins using the pressure cooker allowing him to serve his customers quicker. By 1940 he created his famous Original Recipe. KFC is now is over 80 countries around the world.

KFC Potato Salad

Description: *An easy to prepare home-style potato salad.*

Ingredients

2 pounds russet potatoes
1 cup mayonnaise
4 teaspoons sweet pickle relish
4 teaspoons sugar
2 teaspoons minced white onion
2 teaspoons prepared mustard
1 teaspoon vinegar
1 teaspoon minced celery
1 teaspoon diced pimentos

1-2 teaspoons shredded carrot
1/4 teaspoon dried parsley
1/4 teaspoon pepper
dash salt

RecipeSecrets.net tip:
If you don't have pimientos, use diced red or green bell pepper.

1. Peel potatoes leaving a bit of the skins still on; chop or dice into bite-sized pieces; place in saucepan, cover with water and add salt. Bring to boil and cook until tender. Drain and rinse in cold water; place in large bowl and set aside.

2. Combine remaining ingredients in medium bowl and whisk until smooth and well blended; add to potatoes; mix well.

3. Cover and chill overnight or at least 4 hours before serving.

Makes 6 cups.

Lawry's Seasoned Salt

Description: *Now you can make your own seasoned salt for use on any meat or vegetable dishes.*

Ingredients

2 tablespoons salt
2 teaspoons sugar
1/2 teaspoon paprika
1/4 teaspoon turmeric
1/4 teaspoon onion powder
1/4 teaspoon garlic powder
1/4 teaspoon cornstarch

1. In small bowl, combine and mix well.
2. Store in airtight container if not using right away.

About Lawry's:

Lawry's® makes one of the best seasoned salts on the market today.

Little Caesar's Crazy Sauce

Description: *The perfect blend of spices for a sauce to be used on your pizza or as a dipping sauce for your favorite appetizers.*

Ingredients

15 ounces canned tomato paste
1/2 teaspoon salt
1/4 teaspoon pepper
1/4 teaspoon garlic powder
1/4 teaspoon dried basil
1/4 teaspoon dried marjoram
1/4 teaspoon dried oregano
1/4 teaspoon ground thyme

1. Place saucepan over medium heat; add all ingredients; whisk; blending well.
2. When sauce begins to bubble, reduce heat, simmer for 30 minutes, stirring occasionally. Do not cover during the cooking process.
3. Remove from heat and allow to cool; transfer to covered container and store in refrigerator. This sauce will store, tightly-covered for 3 to 4 weeks.

Makes 1 1/2 cups.

About Little Caesars:

Mike and Marian Ilitch opened their first Little Caesars® restaurant in Garden City, Michigan in 1959. It is now the world's number one carry-out pizza chain selling a wide variety of pizzas, wings and their famous Crazy Bread.

Long John Silver's Hush Puppies

Description: *Enjoy these favorites with your next seafood or chicken dish.*

Ingredients

1/4 cup milk
1 egg
1/2 cup corn meal
1/4 cup flour
1 teaspoon baking powder
1/4 teaspoon garlic
1/2 large onion, minced

RecipeSecrets.net tip:
To make your own baking powder, combine I tablespoon baking soda, 2 tablespoons cream of tartar and I 1/2 tablespoons cornstarch

1. Preheat deep fryer to 350 degrees F.
2. In medium bowl, combine cornmeal, flour, baking powder, and garlic; whisk well to blend.
3. In small bowl, slightly beat egg; add milk; stir; add to dry ingredients. Batter will be thick and should have the consistency of a bread-type batter. If too thin, add a little more cornmeal.
4. Using an ice cream scoop or 2 spoons, drop dough in hot grease and cook until golden on both sides; remove from grease using slotted spoon; drain on paper towels.

Serves 4

About Long John Silver's:

Inspired by the classic Treasure Island, Long John Silver's® was founded in 1969. A quick-service seafood restaurant specializing in serving real meals featuring batter-dipped fish, chicken and shrimp, along with fries, coleslaw and hushpuppies.

Macaroni Grill Bella Napoli

Description: *Deep-fried pasta triangles topped with cream sauce, and sprinkled with sausage, tomatos, peppers, olives and cheeses.*

Ingredients

1/2 pound pasta sheets
oil, for deep-frying
Kalamata olives, sliced
banana peppers, sliced
chopped tomato
1/2 to 1 cup Asiago cheese,
  grated
1 piece cooked Italian sausage
1 piece cooked, sweet Italian
  sausage

Asiago Cream Sauce:
2 cups heavy whipping cream
1/16 teaspoon chicken soup
  base
1/2 cup plus 2 tablespoons
  Asiago cheese
1/2 tablespoon cornstarch
1 ounce water
2 to 3 cups mozzarella cheese

1. Preheat deep fryer to 375 degrees F. Preheat oven to 400 degrees F.
2. Prepare cream sauce: In saucepan, over medium heat, bring cream to very hot temperature - but do not boil; add chicken base and cheese; whisk constantly while bringing the temperature back to just bubbly.
3. In small bowl, dissolve cornstarch in cold water; add to sauce; whisk well. Bring sauce to a slow simmer; simmer for 10 minutes. Remove from heat; cool. Once cooled, sauce can be stored in refrigerator in covered container if making this sauce ahead of time; re-heat to serve.
4. Cut pasta sheets into triangles; place a few at a time in deep fryer (do not crowd); fry until golden; drain on paper towels. Transfer to ovenproof baking dish in layers - half the fried pasta chips, sprinkle with Asiago cheese, top with sauce; another layer of pasta chips, sprinkle with Asiago, top with sausage, tomatoes, peppers, olives, mozzarella and more

Asiago.

5. Place dish on top rack of preheated oven; bake until cheese melts and just begins to brown.

Serves 4

About Romano's Macaroni Grill:

Romano's Macaroni Grill® bills itself as a chain of casual Italian dining restaurants located around the world. The first Romano's Macaroni Grill opened in San Antonio, Texas in 1988 by Phil Romano.

Macaroni Grill Chicken Cannelloni

Description: *Pasta rolls filled with chicken, spinach, ricotta, sun-dried tomatoes and mozzarella smothered in a delicious cannelloni sauce made from Asiago cream sauce combined with tomato sauce.*

Ingredients

12 lasagna pasta sheets, approximate size of 5 x 6 inches

1/2 teaspoon fresh ground black pepper
1 teaspoon salt

Cannelloni Filling:
8 ounces chicken breast (about 2), cooked thoroughly
1 ounce fresh spinach, chopped
1 ounce sun-dried tomatoes, sliced
16 ounces ricotta cheese
3 ounces mozzarella cheese, shredded

Cannelloni Sauce:
16 ounces Asiago cream sauce, or your favorite Alfredo sauce
16 ounces tomato pasta sauce
3 ounces Parmesan cheese, grated

1. Cook chicken thoroughly and cool to an internal temperature of 45 degrees F.; dice into ½-inch pieces and transfer to large bowl.
2. Add spinach, tomatoes, ricotta, mozzarella, pepper and salt; stir thoroughly to combine.
3. Prepare Cannelloni Sauce: In bowl, combine sauces and blend well; set aside.
4. Preheat oven to 350 degrees F.
5. Meanwhile, fill pasta sheets: Place 2 to 3 rounded tablespoons down the center of each sheet; carefully roll cigar fashion and place in baking dish, side by side.
6. Pour sauce over cannelloni, covering completely; sprinkle with Parmesan; cover with foil.

7. Place in preheated oven; bake about 20 minutes; remove foil and continue to bake an additional 20 minutes. If using a thermometer the internal temperature should read 165 degrees F. Remove from oven and serve hot. If desired, garnish dishes with diced tomatoes, basil or Italian parsley.

8. Another favorite is to serve with a dollop of ricotta cheese on the side.

Serves 6

Macaroni Grill Chicken Scaloppini

Description: *Cappellini tossed with pancetta, mushrooms, artichoke hearts and capers in a lemon-butter sauce and topped with chicken.*

Ingredients

6-8 chicken breasts, (3-ounces each) pounded thin
oil & butter for sauteing chicken
2 3/4 cups flour, seasoned with salt and pepper, for dredging
6 oz. pancetta, cooked
12 oz. mushrooms, sliced
12 oz. artichoke hearts, sliced
1 tablespoon capers

1 lb. cappellini pasta, cooked
chopped parsley, for garnish

Lemon Butter Sauce:
4 oz. lemon juice
2 oz. white wine
4 oz. heavy cream
1 lb. butter, (4 sticks)

1. Prepare Lemon Butter Sauce: In small saucepan, combine lemon juice and white wine. Place over medium heat; whisk to combine and bring to boil; reduce by one-third.

2. Add cream, whisking to combine; reduce heat and simmer (never boil cream) until mixture thickens - about 3 to 4 minutes. Gradually add butter, whisking to incorporate after each addition. Season with salt and pepper. Remove from heat; keep warm.

3. Cook pasta until al dente; drain; do not rinse.

4. In large skillet, heat a bit of oil and 2 tablespoons butter. Dredge chicken in flour, shake off excess and place in hot pan. Cook, turning once, until brown and cooked through. Juices should run clear. Remove from pan; set aside.

5. Add remaining ingredients to pan; saute until mushrooms have softened and are cooked; return chicken to pan.

6. Add half of butter sauce to pan; toss to coat; remove from heat.

7. Plate cooked pasta; place chicken over pasta; drizzle with a little more sauce. Serve hot.

Serves 6-8

McDonald's® Cinnamon Melts

Description: *Icing-topped cinnamon rolls for breakfast, brunch or anytime.*

Ingredients

Dough:
2 1/4 teaspoons active dry yeast
1/2 cup warm water (105 - 110 degrees F)
1/2 cup granulated sugar
1/2 cup milk
1/3 cup butter
2 eggs
1 teaspoon salt
4 1/2 - 5 1/2 cups all-purpose flour, divided

Filling:
1 cup packed dark brown sugar
2 tablespoons ground cinnamon
2/3 cup butter, melted

Icing:
1/4 cup butter, softened
1/4 cup cream cheese, softened
1 1/2 cups powdered sugar
1/4 teaspoon vanilla extract
1 tablespoon milk

1. Using a small bowl, dissolve yeast in warm water; let sit 5 minutes.

2. Meanwhile, in large bowl, combine sugar, 1/2 cup milk and 1/3 cup melted butter; add eggs and salt. Add 1 cup flour; blend together. Add second cup of flour. Add proofed yeast. Using a wooden spoon, add remaining flour.

3. Knead on lightly floured surface. Form dough into a ball; place in lightly greased bowl, cover and let rise in warm place for 1 1/2 hours.

4. Next, prepare the filling: combine brown sugar, cinnamon and 2/3 cup melted butter; set aside.

5. After dough has risen, punch down and roll on floured surface to a thickness of ½-inch. Cut in ½-inch wide strips using a sharp knife or a pizza wheel. Slice strips into 3/4 to 1-inch long pieces of dough.

6. Grease large muffin tin cups with softened butter or margarine. Drop 6 chunks of dough into each cup; spoon 1 - 1 ½ teaspoons of cinnamon filling over dough; top with 7 more pieces of dough and sprinkle each cup with 2 more teaspoons cinnamon filling. Cover once again and allow to rise in warm spot for 30 to 45 minutes.

7. Preheat oven to 350 degrees F. Bake in preheated oven for 20 to 30 minutes or until a light golden brown. The bottoms need to be cooked.

8. While still warm, prepare icing. Mix margarine and cream cheese, beating on high speed with mixer; add confectioners' sugar and beat slowly until all incorporated. Add the remaining 1 tablespoon milk and vanilla; mix on high until smooth and fluffy. Spread about 1 tablespoon icing on each cinnamon melt.

Make 1 dozen.

RecipeSecrets.net tip: For a really strong cinnamon flavor, double the cinnamon filling.

About McDonald's:

In 1955, Ray Kloc opened in Des Plaines, Illinois - selling hamburgers for 15 cents. Since then McDonald's® has become the largest and fastest growing fast-food chain in the world.

McDonald's Iced Coffee

Description: This is a low-fat, sugar free and decaf version.

Ingredients

ice cubes
1/4 cup sugar free French Vanilla Coffee Mate
1/2 cup skim milk
1 pkt. Splenda flavors for coffee, French Vanilla

Coffee:
3 scoops decaf coffee
5 cups water

1. Brew coffee and cool completely.
2. To serve: Fill a 16-ounce cup with ice cubes; add Coffee Mate, milk, sweetener and pour in coffee. Stir well. Enjoy.

Serves 1

Michael Jordan's Steak House Chile Rub

Description: *A tangy rub for enhancing your steak's taste. Great for grilling.*

Ingredients

1 tablespoon ancho-chili powder
1 teaspoon ground cumin
1 teaspoon ground coriander
1 teaspoon garlic powder
1 teaspoon cayenne pepper
1 tablespoon kosher salt

1. In small bowl, combine all ingredients, whisking well.
2. Transfer to covered container and store in pantry.
3. To use: Prepare steaks by oiling lightly on both sides; rub 1 teaspoon of chile rub into each side and grill steak to desired doneness.
4. When grilling steaks, be sure to keep the steaks further away from the hot center of the fire - the ancho chili powder does have a tendency to burn.

About Michael Jordan's Steak House:

Michael Jordan retired from basketball and opened his steakhouse in the Grand Central Terminal in New York City in 1997 serving excellent quality steaks cooked to perfection.

Mrs. Fields Peanut Butter Cookies

Description: *Just an old-fashioned favorite drop cookie with that familiar and delicious flavor of peanut butter.*

Ingredients

1/4 teaspoon salt
1/2 teaspoon baking soda
2 cups flour
2 teaspoons vanilla extract
1 cup creamy peanut butter
3 eggs
1 cup softened butter
1 1/4 cup granulated sugar

1 1/4 cup firmly packed dark brown sugar

RecipeSecrets.net tip: Make your own brown sugar my mixing one cup of granulated sugar and one tablespoon of light molasses.

1. Preheat oven to 300 degrees F.
2. In medium bowl, whisk flour, baking soda and salt to combine; set aside.
3. In large bowl, cream butter with mixer at medium speed; add sugar; beat until it forms a paste; add eggs, peanut butter and vanilla extract. Continue beating on medium speed until light and fluffy.
4. With mixer on low speed, gradually add dry ingredients; continue to beat until just mixed.
5. Drop by tablespoonfuls onto ungreased baking sheets placing 1 ½ inches apart. Using the tines of a fork, gently press a criss-cross pattern on top of cookies.

6. Place in preheated oven and bake 10 to 20 minutes until cookies are done and slightly brown around edges; do not overbake.

7. Transfer immediately to wire rack to cool completely. Store airtight.

Serves 8-10

About Mrs. Field's:

Mrs. Fields Cookies® was founded by Debbi Fields, born 1956 in Park City, Utah. She and her husband started their business in the late 1970s, opening the first of many retail bakeries in Palo Alto, California. Mrs. Fields cookies are now commonly sold across the country in grocery stores and malls.

Old Bay Seasoning

Description: *Now you can make your own version of this season-ing which is perfect for crabs, seafood and chicken as well as corn on the cob.*

Ingredients

1 tablespoon ground bay leaves
2 1/2 teaspoons celery salt
1 1/2 teaspoons dry mustard
1 1/2 teaspoons black pepper
3/4 teaspoon ground nutmeg
1/2 teaspoon ground cloves
1/2 teaspoon ground ginger
1/2 teaspoon sweet Hungarian
  paprika

1/2 teaspoon red pepper
1/4 teaspoon ground mace
1/4 teaspoon ground cardamom

1. Combine all ingredients, store in an airtight container.

About Old Bay:

For more than 60 years, Old Bay® Seasoning has been the secret ingredient for cooks from coast to coast. Developed in 1939 by German immigrant Gustav Brunn, who came to America with the goal of starting a famous spice business. He named his famous seasoning after the old steamship line that served passengers and moved cargo in the Chesapeake Bay.

Olive Garden Apple Carmelina

Description: *A delicious apple dessert topped with crumb topping and served with a scoop of vanilla ice cream.*

Ingredients

Filling:
2 (20 ounce) cans sliced apples, drained
1/2 cup granulated sugar
1/2 teaspoon apple pie spice
1/4 cup firmly packed brown sugar
1/4 cup all-purpose flour
1/4 teaspoon salt

Topping:
3/4 cup all-purpose flour
1/4 teaspoon salt
1/2 cup firmly packed brown sugar
1/4 cup granulated sugar
5 tablespoons butter, softened

1. Preheat oven to 350 degrees F. Lightly butter 8-inch square baking dish; set aside.
2. Prepare Topping: In small bowl, combine flour, salt and sugars; blend well; using wide-tined fork, work in softened butter until mixture resembles coarse meal; set aside.
3. Prepare Filling: In medium bowl, combine apples, sugar, apple pie spice, brown sugar, flour and salt; mix well to combine. Pour into prepared pan. Sprinkle topping over apple filling.
4. Place in preheated oven; bake for 30 to 35 minutes or until hot and bubbling and topping is browned.
5. Serve with a scoop of ice cream; drizzle with caramel sauce.

Serves 6

About Olive Garden:

Olive Garden was opened in 1982, specializing in Tuscan foods. Hundreds of Olive Garden team members have traveled to Tuscany to learn how authentic Italian food is prepared and to experience Italy first-hand. Those recipes are served to their devoted customers daily.

Olive Garden Capellini Pomodoro

Description: *An easy no-cook tomato based sauce with basil and garlic tossed with fresh pasta and heated through.*

Ingredients

14 oz capellini pasta (angel hair)
8 medium tomatoes, cut into 1/2" pieces
11 fresh basil leaves, chopped
2 cloves garlic, chopped
6 tablespoons olive oil
salt and freshly ground pepper, to taste
grated Italian cheese for serving

1. In large pot of salted boiling water, cook pasta until al dente (to the bite); drain; do not rinse.
2. Meanwhile, in large bowl, combine diced tomatoes, chopped basil, garlic and oil; season to taste with salt and pepper; whisk to combine.
3. Add pasta to bowl, toss lightly to coat well. Transfer to large saute pan to heat through.
4. Serve immediately. Sprinkle with grated Italian cheese of choice.

Serves 4

Olive Garden Chicken Giardino

Description: *Marinated chicken strips and sautéed vegetables in a delicately seasoned sauce tossed with pasta.*

Ingredients

Sauce:
1 tablespoon butter
1/4 teaspoon dry thyme
1/2 teaspoon fresh rosemary, finely chopped
1 teaspoon garlic pepper
1 tablespoon cornstarch
1/4 cup chicken broth
1/4 cup water
1/4 cup white wine
1 tablespoon milk
1 teaspoon lemon juice
salt and pepper to taste

Chicken:
2 lbs boneless, skinless chicken breasts, sliced width-wise into 1/2" strips
1/4 cup extra-virgin olive oil
2 small rosemary sprigs
1 clove garlic, finely minced
juice of 1/2 lemon

Vegetables:
1/4 cup extra-virgin olive oil
1/2 bunch fresh asparagus (remove bottom inch of stem; cut remainder into 1" pieces)
1 zucchini, julienne cut
1 yellow summer squash, julienne cut
2 Roma tomatoes, cut into 1/2" pieces
1/2 red bell pepper, julienne cut
1 cup broccoli florets, blanched
1/2 cup frozen peas
1 cup spinach, cut into 1/2" pieces
1/2 cup carrots, julienne cut

1 lb farfalle pasta, cooked according to package directions

1. Prepare sauce: In bowl, combine broth, water, wine, milk and lemon juice; whisk well to blend; add cornstarch, whisking until cornstarch is has dissolved completely and mixture is lump-free.

2. Over medium heat, melt butter in saucepan; stir in thyme, garlic pepper and rosemary, whisking to combine; cook for 1 minute. Add broth mixture to pan, whisking; bring to boil. Season to taste with salt and pepper; bring to boil; remove from heat.

3. Cook pasta al dente (to the bite) in large pot of boiling salted water; drain; do not rinse.

4. Meanwhile, prepare chicken: In bowl, combine all chicken ingredients; mix well; cover and refrigerate for 30 minutes.

5. Heat large saute pan over medium-high heat; add ¼ cup olive oil. Saute chicken strips until cooked through; juices will run clear and internal temperature will read 165 degrees F.

6. Add vegetables to saute pan; cook through. Add pasta and sauce to pan; toss gently to coat thoroughly; heat through.

7. Transfer to serving platter; garnish with chopped parsley.

Serves 4

Olive Garden Chicken Marsala

Description: *Lightly coated chicken breasts skillet fried with sauteed mushrooms in a Marsala sauce.*

Ingredients

4 chicken half breasts -
  boneless, skinless
1/4 cup cake flour (Wondra)
1/2 teaspoon salt
1/2 teaspoon oregano
4 tablespoons oil
4 tablespoons butter
1/2 teaspoon pepper
1 cup fresh mushrooms, sliced

1/2 cup Marsala wine

1. In shallow dish, combine flour, salt, pepper and oregano; stir to blend.
2. In heavy skillet, heat oil and butter until butter melts and mixture bubbles lightly.
3. Dredge chicken in seasoned flour; shake off excess; saute in pan 2 minutes for the first side or until lightly browned; as you turn chicken, add mushrooms around the chicken pieces. Cook about 2 more minutes, until lightly browned on the second side; stir mushrooms. Once the second side is lightly browned, add wine around the pieces, cover and simmer for 10 minutes.
4. Transfer to plates and serve.

Serves 4

Olive Garden Chocolate Ricotta Pie

Description: *A creamy ricotta-filled pie dotted with chocolate chips in a graham cracker crust.*

Ingredients

Crust:
1 1/4 cups graham cracker crumbs
2 1/2 ounces melted butter
2 tablespoons granulated sugar

Filling:
1 pound ricotta cheese
3/4 cup confectioners' sugar
1 teaspoon almond extract
1 cup toasted almonds
1/2 cup semisweet chocolate chips
1 1/4 cups heavy cream

1. Prepare crust: In small bowl, combine all ingredients; blend well. Press onto bottom and sides of 9-inch pie pan; place in refrigerator.
2. Prepare filling: In medium bowl, combine ricotta, sugar and extract; blend well; set aside.
3. Chop nuts and chocolate; fold into filling; chill.
4. In large bowl, whip cream until stiff; fold into filling.
5. Spoon filling into chilled crust; spread evenly; refrigerate over night before serving.

Servings: 8

Olive Garden Conchiglie with Tomato & Basil

Description: *Shell pasta smothered in a fresh tomato-basil sauce and topped with Italian cheeses.*

Ingredients

1 1/2 lbs ripe vine tomatoes, peeled, seeded & coarsely diced
8-10 cloves garlic, peeled and finely sliced
1/4 cup red onion, chopped
1/3 cup extra virgin olive oil
2 tablespoons unsalted butter
salt to taste

black pepper to taste
1/4 cups fresh basil, coarse chopped + leaves for garnish
1/4 cup shredded mozzarella cheese
8 oz medium-size shell pasta
imported Parmigiano Reggiano cheese to sprinkle

RecipeSecrets.net tip: When pasta is cooked al dente, there should be a slight resistance in the center of the pasta when it is chewed.

1. Bring large pot of water to boil; add salt; allow to return to rolling boil; add pasta and cook al dente (to the bite); drain; do not rinse.

2. Meanwhile, In skillet, heat olive oil and butter; add garlic and onions; saute over low heat until onions and garlic turn a light golden brown; add diced tomatoes; cook for 5 minutes. Season with salt and pepper to taste. Add chopped basil; stir to combine.

3. Place cooked pasta in soup plate or bowl, top with tomato mixture; sprinkle with fresh grated Parmigiano Reggiano. Garnish with fresh basil leaves and shredded mozzarella. Serve.

Serves 4

Olive Garden Gazpacho Italiano

Description: *A tomato-chicken based soup with a bit of a kick, infused with a fine blend of fresh herbs, chopped cucumber, bell pepper and pasta.*

Ingredients

Soup Base:
28 ounces canned Italian plum tomatoes
1 garlic clove, minced
1/2 cup very finely-chopped mixed herbs
1/2 cup olive oil
3 tablespoons white wine vinegar
3 tablespoons lemon juice
1 teaspoon salt
1/4 cup diced white or red onion
3 cups chicken broth
3/4 teaspoon Tabasco sauce
1 teaspoon sugar (optional)

Pasta and Vegetables:
1/2 cup finely chopped green bell pepper
1/2 cup peeled, finely chopped cucumber
1 cup tomato, cut in 1/4-inch dice
1/2 cup ditalini or tubetti, cooked, rinsed and drained

Garnish:
croutons
freshly-grated Parmesan cheese
chopped fresh parsley

1. Prepare soup base: Using food processor or blender, process tomatoes with juice (do not drain), garlic and herbs. Transfer to non-reactive bowl and add olive oil, vinegar, lemon juice, salt, onion, stock, Tabasco and sugar. Cover and place in refrigerator allowing 4 hours for soup base to chill and flavors to blend.
2. Prepare vegetables and cook pasta. Chill in refrigerator.
3. Place bowls in refrigerator to chill; they should be very cold.
4. To serve: Stir base very well; ladle 6 ounces into chilled bowl; add a large tablespoon of vegetables and 2 tablespoons pasta to bowl.
5. Garnish with a couple croutons that have been sprinkled with Parmesan cheese and chopped parsley.

NOTE: This soup is served cold - at a temperature of 35 to 45 degrees. Do not add vegetables and pasta solids to base until time of serving or they will be soggy and unenjoyable.

Serves 6

Olive Garden Neapolitan Ziti

Description: *Ziti pasta with Italian sausage and bell peppers smothered in marinara sauce.*

Ingredients

1 1/2 pounds sweet/hot Italian
link sausage
1 1/3 cups green bell pepper in
1/4-inch strips
2 tablespoons olive oil
3/4 pound ziti pasta, cooked
grated Parmesan cheese
parsley bouquets

Marinara Sauce:
1 (28 ounce) can Italian-style or
plum tomatoes with juice
10 3/4 ounces tomato puree
1 teaspoon minced garlic
4 tablespoons olive oil
1/2 cup chopped fresh basil
(packed)
salt, to taste
freshly-ground black pepper, to
taste

1. Fully cook sausages by skillet frying or by baking; drain; cool and cut in half lengthwise; cut each half into ½-inch slices.
2. Meanwhile, bring large pot of water to boil, cook pasta until al dente (to the bite); drain; do not rinse.
3. While preparing pasta, in skillet, heat olive oil over moderate heat. Add peppers and saute just until they lose their crispness but are not soft.
4. Meanwhile, in heavy saucepan, heat olive oil; add tomatoes, tomato puree, garlic, and fresh basil; bring to light simmer over moderate heat. Add pepper strips and cooked sausage; heat for 3 to 5 minutes.
5. Serve pasta, topped with sausage mixture and sauce. Garnish with parsley and serve with extra grated Parmesan cheese.

Serves 4

Olive Garden Pepperoni Pasta Palermo

Description: *Rigatoni with a medley of roasted bell peppers, pepperoni, and garlic in an Italian seasoned herbed vinaigrette with tomatoes, olives, sun-dried tomatoes, and pistachios - topped with Parmesan.*

Ingredients

1 pound rigatoni (large size)
1 red bell pepper
1 yellow bell pepper
1 green bell pepper
2 ounces thinly sliced pepperoni,
  divided use (cut 1 oz. in strips,
  leave 1 oz. sliced)
1/2 cup garlic cloves
1 teaspoon olive oil
herbed vinaigrette dressing
1 large tomato, chopped
1/2 cup Kalamata olives, cut in
  half

1/2 cup sun-dried tomatoes,
  sliced
1 tablespoon capers, rinsed
1 teaspoon chopped fresh
  rosemary
1/2 teaspoon salt
black pepper, to taste
1/4 cup fresh basil leaves, cut in
  strips
1/4 cup pistachios, roughly
  chopped
Parmesan cheese shavings, for
  garnish

1. In large pot of boiling water, cook pasta according to package directions; rinse with cold water; drain; refrigerate.
2. Preheat oven to 450 degrees F.
3. Using grill or broiler, roast peppers, charring skins well. Place in paper sack, plastic bag or in bowl covered tightly with plastic wrap to allow to sweat. When cool enough to handle, remove charred skin using a paring knife; discard charred skins. Julienne skinned peppers into strips.
4. Meanwhile, coat garlic cloves with olive oil and roast in preheated oven for 5 to 10 minutes; cool.
5. In large mixing bowl combine vinaigrette, chopped tomato, rigatoni, peppers, garlic cloves, pepperoni strips, olives, sun-dried tomatoes, capers, rosemary,

salt and pepper.

6. Refrigerate 2 hours or overnight.

7. To serve: Place pasta in large serving bowl; add fresh cut basil and pistachio nuts; toss lightly.

8. Garnish with sliced pepperoni, fresh basil and shaved Parmesan. Serve immediately.

Serves 6-8

Olive Garden Ravioletti in Mushroom-Walnut Cream Sauce

Description: *A creamy Parmesan sauce over ravioletti, sauteed mushrooms and walnuts.*

Ingredients

12 ounces ravioletti or tricolored tortellini, cooked
2 tablespoons extra-virgin olive oil
8 ounces mushrooms, sliced
1/4 cup walnuts, chopped
3/4 cup heavy whipping cream
1/4 teaspoon freshly-ground black pepper

2 cups freshly-grated Parmesan cheese

1. In large skillet, over medium heat, add olive oil to skillet and heat; add mushrooms and walnuts; saute until golden; add cream; cook, stirring frequently 5 minutes or until lightly thickened.
2. Reduce heat to medium and allow to simmer; do not boil cream. Add pepper and Parmesan; stir smooth.
3. Serve hot cooked pasta with sauce.

Serves 4

Olive Garden Seafood Torcello

Description: *Cod, crab and shrimp in a clam-sherry sauce over pasta.*

Ingredients

1 pound cod fillets
6 ounces clams, drained and chopped
6 ounces rock shrimp, cooked
6 ounces crabmeat, picked over
6 ounces dry radiatore, spirelli or pasta, cooked

Bechamel Sauce:
3 tablespoons butter
3 1/2 tablespoons all-purpose flour
2 cups whole milk
1/2 teaspoon salt
2 tablespoons olive oil
2 teaspoons garlic, minced
1/2 cup straight sherry, not dry
1 tablespoon parsley, chopped
2 quarts boiling salted water

1. Preheat oven to 400 degrees F. Line baking sheet with foil; spray foil with cooking spray.

2. Place cod fillets on prepared baking sheet and bake, uncovered, for 5 to 6 minutes, only until the cod flakes easily. Immediately remove from oven to prevent overcooking. Cool, break filets in half lengthwise; break each half into 1-inch pieces; set aside.

3. Meanwhile, bring large pot of water to boil, cook pasta, drain; do not rinse.

4. While preparing pasta, in heavy non-reactive 3-quart pot (not aluminum), melt butter over moderate heat; add flour and cook 3 minutes, whisking constantly. Do not allow flour to brown. Add milk and salt; bring to just below boiling point, whisking constantly - do not boil milk. Remove from heat; keep warm at 180 degrees F.

5. Meanwhile, place oil in saute pan and heat over medium heat; add garlic and saute only until white throughout; transfer garlic to sauce.

6. Pour sherry into saute pan garlic was in; simmer strongly for 1 minute; transfer to warm sauce.

7. Add cooked pasta to sauce; return saucepan to low heat for a few minutes; add cooked cod, clams, shrimp, crabmeat and chopped parsley. Heat through; serve immediately.

Serves 4-6

Olive Garden Sicilian Scampi

Description: *Large shrimp sauteed in extra-virgin olive oil with white wine, garlic and lemon*

Ingredients

6 pieces fan tail shrimp (uncooked)
1/8 cup olive oil
1 tablespoon onion, finely diced
1/2 teaspoon minced garlic
1/2 cup white wine (Chablis)
1 tablespoon flour (mix with 1 tablespoon water)
2 tablespoons fresh lemon juice
1/4 teaspoon garlic salt
1/2 cup heavy cream
1/4 cup water, if sauce is too thick
1/2 cup plus 1 tablespoon

Asiago cheese, finely shredded
1/4 cup mozzarella cheese, finely shredded
1 tablespoon Romano cheese, finely shredded
4 black olives, sliced
1 tablespoon green onion, sliced
1/4 cup diced tomato
4 slices Italian bread
1/4 teaspoon crushed red pepper
grated Parmesan cheese, to serve

1. Place olive in saucepan and heat over medium heat; add wine and lemon juice; when mixture begins to boil, add shrimp; cook until shrimp curls and are cooked through; remove shrimp from pan to dish.

2. Add onion, garlic and garlic salt to pan and saute until onions are transparent; do not brown. Add flour and water paste; whisk; cooking until thick.

3. Add cream; whisk; add cheeses, one at a time, whisking constantly after each addition. Sauce should have a medium-thick consistency and smooth. If the sauce is too thick, add a little water; whisk to blend well. Remove from heat.

4. Place 2 slices Italian bread on serving dish, criss-crossing. Arrange shrimp in the middle of bread; spoon sauce over shrimp; sprinkle with sliced green

onions, olives and tomatoes. Top with a sprinkle of crushed red pepper and Parmesan cheese.

Serves 2

Olive Garden Tortelloni Bolognese

Description: *Tortelloni tossed in a traditional meat and sausage sauce.*

Ingredients

2 tablespoons olive oil
1 onion, finely chopped
1 carrot, finely chopped
1 celery stalk, finely chopped
2 garlic cloves, finely chopped
1/2 lb ground beef
6 oz Italian sausage, skinned
1 cup red wine
18 oz can crushed tomatoes,
  chopped

1 teaspoon fresh rosemary,
  chopped (1/4 teaspoon dry)
1 teaspoon fresh sage, chopped
  (1/4 teaspoon dry)
salt to taste
pepper to taste
2 lbs tortelloni
Parmesan cheese, freshly grated

RecipeSecrets.net tip: Substitute ground turkey and turkey sausage for a healthy alternative.

1. In large heavy skillet, heat oil; add celery, carrot, onion and garlic; cook for 5 minutes. Add meat; cook over medium heat for 10 minutes, stirring occasionally.

2. Pour wine into pan to de-glaze. Reduce. Add tomatoes and remaining ingredients; stir to combine. Simmer for one hour.

3. Half way through simmering time, bring large pot of water to boil; cook pasta; drain; do not rinse.

4. Transfer hot pasta to serving platter; pour sauce over; toss to coat. Top with Parmesan cheese. Serve immediately.

Serves 6

Outback Steakhouse Coconut Shrimp

Description: *Battered, rolled in coconut and deep fried shrimp served with a sweet and sour sauce.*

Ingredients

1 1/2 lb large raw shrimp	oil for deep frying
1/2 cup all-purpose flour	2 cups short shredded coconut
1/2 cup cornstarch	1/2 cup orange marmalade
1 tablespoon salt	1/4 cup Grey Poupon Mustard
1/2 tablespoon white pepper	1/4 cup honey
2 tablespoons vegetable oil	3-4 drops Tabasco sauce
1 cup ice water	

1. Preheat oven to 300 degrees F.
2. Heat oil in deep fryer or electric skillet to 350 degrees F.
3. Prepare dipping sauce: Combine marmalade, mustard, honey and Tabasco sauce; mix well; cover and refrigerate.
4. Peel and devein shrimp; wash well; dry on paper towels; set aside.
5. In medium bowl, combine dry ingredients for batter; whisk well to blend. Add 2 tablespoons oil and ice water; whisk well to blend.
6. Place coconut in shallow dish. Dip shrimp in batter; allow excess to drain off; roll in coconut; fry in hot oil until lightly browned; about 4 minutes. Remove from hot oil and transfer to baking pan; place in preheated oven and bake for 5 minutes to finish cooking.
7. Serve with dipping sauce or sweet and sour sauce.

Serves 4-6

About Outback Steakhouse:

Outback® was founded in Florida in 1987. At the time, the 1986 movie Crocodile Dundee had become a big hit. The Outback was kind of the wild, wild west of Australia. So they brought the Australian western theme to the restaurant.

Outback Steakhouse Steak Marinade

Description: *Perfectly brewed Scottish ale makes this a great marinade for any steaks.*

Ingredients

1 cup Scottish Ale
2 teaspoons brown sugar
1/2 teaspoon seasoned salt
1/4 teaspoon ground black pepper
1/4 teaspoon Accent

RecipeSecrets.net tip:
Accent is a flavor enhancer sold in the spice section of most supermarkets.

1. Place favorite cut of steak in shallow baking pan; pour ale over; cover; refrigerate for 1 hour, turning steak occasionally.

2. In small bowl, combine dry ingredients; mix well and transfer to shallow dish.

3. Remove steak from marinade; discard marinade. Press steak into dry ingredients, coating both sides. Rub seasoning in well using fingers. Place back in dish on top of dry mixture; cover with plastic wrap; refrigerate for 30 minutes, turning occasionally.

4. Preheat grill or add butter to skillet and melt; when butter bubbles, add steak to skillet (or place on grill) and cook to desired doneness.

This recipe makes enough marinade for 1 ½ pounds of beef.

P. F. Chang's China Bistro BBQ Sauce

Description: *Chang's BBQ Sauce for beef, ribs or chicken.*

Ingredients

3 cups Heinz ketchup
1 1/2 cups sugar
2 1/2 oz Kikkoman Soy Sauce
2 oz Junmai Ginjo sake
2 oz water
1 1/2 oz. Hoisin sauce
2 teaspoons five spice powder
1 teaspoon finely minced
  ginger root

1 teaspoon finely minced garlic
1 teaspoon ground star anise

RecipeSecrets.net tip: Hoisin sauce is made from soybean paste and flavored with garlic, sugar, chillies and other spices.

1. In large bowl, combine all ingredients; whisk well until sugar has dissolved.
2. Store in refrigerator in covered container.

Makes 1 quart.

About P. F. Chang's China Bistro:

P. F. Chang's® is unique. It blends classic Chinese design with a modern bistro look. Each location features an original handpainted mural depicting scenes of life in 12th century China. The goal of a P. F. Chang's meal is to attain harmony of taste, texture, color and aroma.

P. F. Chang's China Bistro Cellophane Noodle Salad

Description: *Cellophane noodles with shrimp and julienned vegetables tossed in a Chinese vinaigrette.*

Ingredients

8 ounces bean threads
(cellophane noodles)
1/2 pound cooked, peeled and
deveined shrimp
julienned green onions, carrots
and cucumber for garnish
chopped cilantro for garnish

Dressing:
6 tablespoons soy sauce
6 tablespoons rice vinegar
2 tablespoons oyster sauce
6 teaspoons chili garlic sauce
3 teaspoons sesame oil
2 teaspoons granulated sugar

RecipeSecrets.net tip:
Parsley can be substituted
for cilantro in this recipe.

1. Bring medium pot of water to boil.

2. Meanwhile, soak bean threads in warm water until soft, about 15 minutes. Cut into 4-inch lengths; transfer to boiling water and cook for 1 minute; remove; drain; cool and pat dry.

3. In bowl, combine dressing ingredients; blend well. Add noodles; toss to coat completely.

4. Place noodles on serving plates in mounds; garnish with shrimp, julienned green onions, carrots, cucumber, and bean sprouts. Garnish with chopped cilantro. Serve.

Serves 4

P. F. Chang's China Bistro Mongolian Beef

Description: *A tasty and flavorful stir-fry dish of beef, rice and vegetables.*

Ingredients

1 lb flank steak
1/4 cup cornstarch
1 cup vegetable oil
2 large green onions, sliced

Sauce:
2 teaspoons vegetable oil
1/2 teaspoon minced ginger
1 tablespoon chopped garlic
1/2 cup soy sauce
1/2 cup water
3/4 cup firmly packed dark
  brown sugar

1. Prepare sauce: Heat 2 teaspoons oil in medium saucepan over medium-low heat. Add ginger and garlic; immediately add soy sauce and water before the garlic scorches. Add brown sugar and dissolve completely; increase heat to medium and bring to a boil; boil for 2 to 3 minutes to thicken; remove from heat.

2. Slice flank steak at an angle against the grain into bit-sized pieces - about ¼-inch thick and dip lightly in cornstarch. Let sit for 10 minutes to allow cornstarch to stick to beef.

3. Meanwhile, heat 1 cup oil in skillet or wok, over medium heat until hot. Add beef and saute for a couple minutes or until beef just begins to darken around the edges; stir. Using a slotted spoon, remove from oil and drain on paper towels; pour hot oil into ceramic bowl.

4. Return skillet to heat, return meat to pan and simmer for a minute or two.

5. Add sauce, cook for one minute, stirring; add green onions. Cook for one more minute; using slotted spoon, remove to serving plate.

Serves 4

RecipeSecrets.net tip: This dish freezes well. Thaw in refrigerator and heat quickly in a skillet.

P. F. Chang's China Bistro Shrimp Dumplings

Description: *Steamed wontons filled with a combination of shrimp, carrot and onion, served with a soy-based dipping sauce.*

Ingredients

1 package wonton wrappers
1 lb peeled and deveined
   medium shrimp, washed and
   dried
2 tablespoons finely minced
   carrot
2 tablespoons finely minced
   green onion
1 teaspoon minced fresh ginger
2 tablespoons oyster sauce
1/4 teaspoon sesame oil

Sauce:
1 cup soy sauce
1 oz white vinegar
1/2 teaspoon chili paste
1 oz sugar
1/2 teaspoon minced fresh
   ginger
sesame oil, to taste
1 cup water
1 tablespoon cilantro leaves

RecipeSecrets.net tip:
Chili paste is an Asian seasoning made from crushed red chilis.

1. Prepare sauce: Combine all ingredients in bowl; whisk well to combine; cover; refrigerate.
1. Place ½ lb. shrimp in food processor and mince fine; transfer to bowl; set aside.
2. Dice remaining shrimp small; add to bowl. Add remaining ingredients; mix well.
3. Fill wontons with a small amount of filling; moisten outside edge; fold corner to corner; seal. Place on plate, cover and refrigerate until ready to cook.
4. When ready to cook, fill saucepan with water; bring to rolling boil; reduce heat; water should be at a slight boil.

5. Line bottom of Chinese steamer with light coating of vegetable oil or non-stick cooking spray. Place dumplings in steamer. Cover and steam 7 to 10 minutes. Dumplings should be firm. If using a cooking thermometer, dumplings should be 160 degrees F.

6. Transfer to serving dish with dipping sauce.

Serves 6

P. F. Chang's China Bistro Spare Ribs

Description: *Tender grilled spareribs in PF Chang's BBQ Sauce.*

Ingredients

5 lbs. pork spareribs
1/3 cup ketchup
3 tablespoons sugar
1 teaspoon salt
2 teaspoons minced garlic
1/3 cup soy sauce
1/3 cup hoisin sauce

1. Place ribs in large pot of water; bring water to simmer; simmer 45 minutes; drain; transfer to dish; cool.
2. In bowl, combine remaining ingredients; whisk to mix well; pour over ribs, turning to coat well; cover; refrigerate overnight.
3. To cook: Bake or grill until done and tender; approximately 30 minutes.

Serves 6

Pappadeaux Seafood Kitchen Alexander Sauce

Description: *A creamy seafood sauce that goes very well with salmon and other seafood dishes. Try it with pasta.*

Ingredients

6 tablespoons unsalted butter, divided
1/2 cup chopped sweet or yellow onion
1 1/2 tablespoons flour
1/2 cup clam juice

2 cups whipping cream
1/2 teaspoon salt
1/4 teaspoon white pepper
1 cup uncooked small shrimp
5 ounces white lump crabmeat
dash of cayenne pepper, optional

1. In large saucepan, melt 3 tablespoons butter; add onion and cook until soft but not browned.
2. Stir in flour; cook 2 minutes, whisking constantly.
3. Gradually pour in clam juice and cream; season with salt, pepper and cayenne. Cook, stirring, about 3 minutes.
4. In saute pan, melt remaining butter; add shrimp; cook for 2 minutes; add crab meat; cook an additional minute; stir into creamed mixture. Combine. Serve hot.

Serves 4

About Pappadeaux Seafood Kitchen:

D. Pappas came to America from Greece in 1897 and opened restaurants throughout Tennessee, Arkansas and Texas. In 1976 his sons opened their first restaurant. There are locations in Houston, Dallas, Chicago, Atlanta, Denver, Phoenix, Austin, San Antonio, and Beaumont and are known for outstanding food and service. Their restaurant family now includes over 60 locations that have been voted Best Seafood, Best Cajun, Favorite Mexican, and Best Steakhouse in local and regional publications year after year by their guests and industry peers.

Perkins Family Restaurant Potato Pancakes

Description: *Perfectly seasoned potato pancakes sauteed in butter. Served with sour cream.*

Ingredients

1 cup all-purpose flour
1 cup whole milk
4 eggs
3 tablespoons butter, melted
3 tablespoons sugar
1/4 teaspoon baking powder
1/2 teaspoon salt
1 tablespoon chopped fresh
  parsley

1 tablespoon minced onion
4 shredded fresh potatoes -or-
2 1/2 cups frozen hash
  browns, defrosted

1. In large bowl, combine all ingredients, except potatoes; beat by hand until mixture is smooth. Add potatoes; mix by hand until well combined.
2. Let mixture rest for 15 minutes.
3. Preheat griddle to medium heat. Grease with butter.
4. Ladle ¼-cup scoops onto heated griddle. Cook about 2 minutes, until brown, turn and cook second side. Serve hot with applesauce or sour cream.

Serves 6

About Perkins Family Restaurant:

With nearly 500 locations in 35 states, Perkins® tantalizes with in-house bake shops while featuring breakfast, lunch and dinner menus from traditional to innovative. Fresh muffins, pies and cookies can top off a meal or be taken out for later.

Pizza Hut Creamy Italian Dressing

Description: *This creamy dressing has just the right amount of herbs and cheese enhancing the flavor of your favorite salads.*

Ingredients

2 teaspoons dried oregano
2 teaspoons dried basil
1/2 teaspoon dried thyme
1/2 teaspoon dried rosemary
1 teaspoon salt
1/2 teaspoon coarsely ground
  black pepper
1/4 cup red wine vinegar

1 tablespoon fresh lemon juice
1/4 cup mayonnaise
3/4 cup extra-virgin olive oil
1/3 cup freshly grated Parmesan
  cheese

RecipeSecrets.net tip:
This also makes a great dipping sauce.

1. In bowl, combine oregano, basil, thyme and rosemary; crush with mortar or crumble in hands. Add salt, pepper, vinegar and lemon juice. Whisk to combine.
2. Add mayonnaise; whisk well. Continue whisking and drizzle in olive oil, whisking until incorporated.
3. Stir in Parmesan.
4. Transfer to jar with tight-fitting lid; store in refrigerator. Shake well before using.

Serves 6

About Pizza Hut:

Pizza Hut® was founded in 1958 by Frank Carney in Topeka, Kansas. The menu includes various pizzas, pastas, salads and more.

Pizza Hut Original Pan Pizza

Description: *The crisp exterior and spongy interior crust with just the right toppings to create this famous pizza. A soft, light and delicious dish.*

Ingredients

1 1/3 cups warm water (105 degrees F)
1/4 cup non-fat dry milk
1/2 teaspoon salt
4 cups flour
1 tablespoon sugar
1 package dry yeast
2 tablespoons vegetable oil (for dough)

9 oz. vegetable oil (3 oz. per pan)
butter flavored cooking spray

Sauce:
1 8 ounce can tomato sauce
1 teaspoon dry oregano
1/2 teaspoon marjoram
1/2 teaspoon dry basil
1/2 teaspoon garlic salt

Toppings:
shredded mozzarella
pepperoni, sausage, vegetables, olives, peppers, onions, etc.

1. Pour 3 oz. vegetable oil into each of three 9-inch round cake pans; spread evenly; set aside.
2. In large bowl, place yeast, sugar and dry milk. Add water; stir to mix well; allow to rest for 2 minutes. Add oil; stir to combine. Add flour and salt; stir until dough forms and flour is absorbed.
3. Turn dough out onto lightly floured, smooth surface and knead 1 minutes; divide dough into 3 pieces using a sharp knife.
4. Roll one piece of dough at a time into a 9-inch circle; place in prepared cake pans.
5. Spray outer edge of dough with cooking spray; cover each pan with a plate; place in warm area and allow to rise for 1 to 1 ½ hours. Place a large towel over the plates to prevent any drafts from effecting dough.
6. Place ingredients for sauce in bowl; whisk well to blend; cover and refrigerate for one hour. Remove

from refrigerator 15 to 30 minutes before baking pizza.

For Each Nine Inch Pizza:

1. Preheat oven to 475 degrees F. For each pizza:
2. Spread 1/3 cup sauce over dough and using the back of a large spoon, spread to within 1-inch of edge.
3. Evenly sprinkle 1 1/2 ounces shredded mozzarella cheese over sauce.
4. Place toppings of choice over cheese. Pepperoni, vegetables, cooked meats (cooked ground sausage or beef) would be placed over cheese in that order.
5. Sprinkle 3 ounces (additional) mozzarella over additional toppings.
6. Bake in preheated oven until cheese is bubbling and outer crust is brown.
7. Using pizza wheel, cut into 6 or 8 wedges.

Makes 3 9-inch pizzas.

Planet Hollywood Pot Stickers

Description: *Deep-fried wonton wrappers filled with ground turkey, ginger, onions and water chestnuts.*

Ingredients

1/4 pound ground turkey
1/2 teaspoon minced fresh
  ginger
1 teaspoon minced green onion
1 teaspoon minced water
  chestnuts
1/2 teaspoon soy sauce
1/2 teaspoon ground black
  pepper

1/4 teaspoon crushed red
  pepper flakes
1/4 teaspoon salt
1/8 teaspoon garlic powder
1 egg, beaten
vegetable oil for frying
12 wonton wrappers (3 x 3-inch
  size)

RecipeSecrets.net tip: Serve with hoisin sauce for dipping.

1. Preheat deep fryer to 375 degrees F. or heat 1 to 2 inches of oil in heavy skillet - just enough to cover pot stickers.
2. Beat egg in small bowl; set aside.
3. In small bowl, combine turkey, ginger, green onion, water chestnuts, soy sauce, peppers, salt, and garlic powder; mix well to blend. Add 1 tablespoon beaten egg. (The remaining egg will be used later).
4. Using a round cookie cutter or an inverted glass with a 3-inch diameter, cut the centers of wonton wrappers to make circles.
5. Spoon ½ tablespoon of turkey mixture into center of wonton wrapper; brush a little remaining beaten egg around half the edge of wrapper; fold over wrapper,

gathering as you seal making a crinkled edge. Repeat with all wrappers.

6. Fry pot stickers, a few at a time, in hot oil for 5 minutes or until browned; drain on paper towels.

4 Servings

About Planet Hollywood:

Planet Hollywood® is another great theme restaurant focusing on movie and Hollywood memorabilia.

Red Lobster Black and Blue Talapia

Description: *Blackened seasoning coats butter brushed tilapia that is covered with bleu cheese.*

Ingredients

tilapia (or salmon, grouper, halibut, sea bass, swordfish)
3 1/2 ounces blue cheese salad dressing, store bought
1/2 cup butter, separated
parsley, chopped
lemon wedge, for garnish
blackened fish seasoning

1. Place talapia filets, darkest or skin-side down in pie plate or shallow dish. Brush with melted butter. This is the presentation side.
2. Season heavily with blackened fish seasoning.
3. Brush skillet with melted butter; carefully flip seasoned filet into skillet; brush dark side of filet with melted butter.
4. Place skillet over medium-high heat; halfway through cooking, carefully flip and continue cooking until internal temperature of fish is 150 degrees F.
5. Garnish with fresh chopped parsley and lemon wedge. Serve with bleu cheese dressing.

Serves 1-2

About Red Lobster:

In 1968 Bill Darden opened the first Red Lobster in Lakeland, Florida. By the early 1970's the company had expanded throughout the southeast United States making them the leader in seafood and casual dining. The chain continues to grow and today has more than 680 restaurants.

Red Lobster Chocolate Lava Cakes

Description: *A warm chocolate cake with a soft, moist center.*

Ingredients

nonstick cooking spray
6 (1 ounce) squares semisweet
  chocolate, coarsely chopped
10 tablespoons unsalted butter,
  at room temperature
1/2 cup granulated sugar
1/2 cup flour
3 tablespoons unsweetened
  cocoa powder
3/4 teaspoon baking powder
3 large eggs, at room
  temperature

1 (10 ounce) package frozen
  raspberries thawed, pureed in
  blender
fresh raspberries, optional
1/2 cup heavy cream, softly
  beaten
fresh mint sprigs, optional
confectioners' sugar for dusting

RecipeSecrets.net tip:
Make your own confection-
ers' sugar: Combine 2 cups
granulated sugar and 4 tablespoons cornstarch in a
blender until powdery.

1. Spray inside of 6 individual souffle dishes or custard cups with nonstick cooking spray; set aside.

2. Over low heat, in small heavy saucepan, melt chocolate, stirring until smooth; add butter and sugar; stir until butter is melted and sugar has dissolved.

3. Transfer to large bowl.

4. In small bowl, combine flour, cocoa and baking powder; whisk well to combine.

5. With electric mixer, beat chocolate mixture at medium-high heat; add eggs, one at a time, beating well after each addition; add dry ingredients; beat until thickened, about 5 or 6 minutes.

6. Divide mixture evenly among prepared dishes; cover with plastic wrap; place in freezer for at least 2 hours or overnight.

7. When ready to bake, preheat oven to 375 degrees F. Remove from freezer; discard plastic wrap. Place on baking sheet and bake 15 to 18 minutes or until edges are set and center is moist.

8. Cool slightly before carefully inverting onto serving plates.

9. Drizzle with raspberry puree; sprinkle with confectioners' sugar; top with whipped cream; and garnish with mint leaves.

Serves: 6

Red Lobster Pina Colada Shrimp

Description: *Battered shrimp that is coated with bread crumbs and coconut, then deep-fried until golden brown. Served with a pina colada dipping sauce.*

Ingredients

6 to 8 cups canola or vegetable oil (for use in the fryer)
12 large shrimp, peeled and deveined
1 1/2 cups all-purpose flour, divided
2 tablespoons granulated sugar
1/4 teaspoon salt
1 cup milk
2 tablespoons Captain Morgan's Parrot Bay Coconut Rum

1 cup panko Japanese bread crumbs
1/2 cup shredded

Pina Colada Dipping Sauce:
1/2 cup sour cream
1/4 cup pina colada mix
1/4 cup crushed pineapple (canned)
2 tablespoons granulated sugar

RecipeSecrets.net tip:
Serve with fresh salsa on the side.

1. Prepare dipping sauce; In small bowl, combine all ingredients and mix well. Cover and refrigerate.

2. Heat oil in deep fryer or in large heavy skillet to 350 degrees F.

3. In medium bowl, place ¾ cup flour.

4. In separate medium bowl, place remaining flour, sugar and salt; whisk to combine; stir in milk and rum. Let stand for 5 minutes.

5. In another bowl, combine panko bread crumbs and shredded coconut; mix well.

6. Butterfly peeled shrimp leaving tail on. Dip each shrimp into plain flour, shake off excess; dip in batter, shake off excess; dip in breadcrumb mixture. Place on plate until all shrimp are ready to fry.

7. Place shrimp in hot oil, one at a time, frying a few at a time, until golden. Remove and drain on paper towels.
8. Serve with dipping sauce.

Serves 2

Red Lobster Tartar Sauce

Description: *A creamy and perfect blend of ingredients for your seafood dishes and sandwiches.*

Ingredients

1/3 cup Miracle Whip salad dressing
2/3 cup sour cream
1/4 cup confectioners' sugar
3 tablespoons sweet white onion, chopped fine
2 tablespoons sweet pickle relish
3 teaspoons carrot, minced
1/4 teaspoon salt

1. Place onion in food processor; chop; transfer to small bowl; set aside.
2. Place carrot in food processor; chop; add to onion.
3. Combine remaining ingredients in separate bowl; whisk well to combine. Add onion and carrot; mix well. Cover; refrigerate at least 2 hours to allow flavors to meld.

Makes 1 cup.

Red Robin BBQ Chicken Salad

Description: *Crisp greens topped with tomato, barbecued chicken, black beans, cheese, bacon, sliced avocado and crunchy French fried onion straws. Served with Ranch dressing.*

Ingredients

2 cups chopped romaine lettuce
2 cups chopped green leaf or
 iceberg lettuce
1/2 cup chopped red cabbage
1 small tomato, chopped (1/4
 cup)
1 boneless skinless chicken
 breast half
1/2 cup barbecue sauce (Bull's
 Eye or K.C. Masterpiece)

1/2 cup refried black beans
1/2 cup shredded Cheddar
 cheese
1/4 cup French's French Fried
 Onions (onion straws)
3 avocado slices (1/4 avocado)
1/4 cup Ranch dressing

1. Preheat grill. Place chicken on grill, brushing generously with barbecue sauce once the chicken is half cooked. Continue to brush with sauce as chicken grills.
2. Combine lettuce and cabbage; arrange on serving plate and top with tomato.
3. In saute pan, heat beans; spread over lettuce on one side of plate.
4. Slice cooked chicken and spread on other side of lettuce on plate.
5. Sprinkle with cheese, top with onions.
6. Garnish with avocado slices; serve with Ranch dressing and remaining barbecue sauce on the side.

Serves 1

About Red Robin:

Red Robin® first opened their doors in Seattle, Washington in 1969. Their focus is on serving an imaginative selection of high-quality gourmet burgers in a family-friendly atmosphere.

Red Robin Mountain-High Mudd Pie

Description: *A special creation of chocolate and vanilla ice cream, peanut butter cookie bits, chopped peanuts, fudge & peanut butter served over chocolate fudge & caramel.*

Ingredients

6 cups chocolate ice cream
1 cup peanut butter cookie
  pieces
6 cups vanilla ice cream
1 2/3 cups creamy peanut
  butter
4 chocolate graham crackers
1 cup fudge topping
1 – 20 oz bottle chocolate syrup

1 – 20 oz bottle caramel syrup
1 can whipped cream
3/4 cup chopped peanuts
12 maraschino cherries, with
  stems

RecipeSecrets.net tip:
Use frozen yogurt or fat-free ice cream.

1. Soften chocolate ice cream; transfer to 3 - 3 ½-quart mixing bowl; smooth top; spread with peanut butter cookie pieces; cover; place in freezer for 1 to 2 hours.
2. Soften vanilla ice cream; spread evenly over cookie topped ice cream; cover; return to freezer for 1 to 2 hours.
3. Spread 2/3 cup peanut butter over surface of ice cream; sprinkle with crushed chocolate graham crackers; cover; return to freezer and freeze for another 1 to 2 hours.
4. Remove bowl from freezer; hold in hot pot of water just long enough to soften around the edges. Invert onto plate; cover with plastic wrap and return to freezer for 2 hours.

5. Remove from freezer; pour fudge topping over ice cream; spread evenly over entire surface; return to freezer for 1 hour.

6. Spread remaining 1 cup peanut butter over surface; drizzle with 1 cup fudge topping; return to freezer for 1 hour.

7. To serve; drizzle serving plate with chocolate and caramel sauces. Using warm knife, cut ice cream in slices and place slice on top of sauces. Top with whipped cream; sprinkle with chopped nuts; place a cherry on top.

Serves 12

Ruby Tuesday Apple Pie

Description: *An easy way to dress-up a frozen pie and intensify the flavor.*

Ingredients

1 (9-inch) frozen deep-dish apple pie
1 stick butter
1 cup light brown sugar, firmly packed, divided
3 1/2 teaspoons cinnamon, divided
1/4 teaspoon allspice
1/4 teaspoon ground clove

1 1/2 teaspoon lemon juice
3/4 cup flour
1/2 cup sugar
10 tablespoon frozen butter
1/3 cup chopped walnuts
ice cream (optional)

1. Remove frozen pie from box and place on wire rack to thaw at room temperature 30 to 45 minutes.
2. Preheat oven to 350 degrees F.
3. Melt stick of butter in small saucepan over medium heat; add ½ cup brown sugar, 1 ½ tablespoons cinnamon, allspice, cloves and lemon juice. Whisk to combine until sugar is dissolved, about 3 minutes. Remove from heat; cool completely.
4. With sharp knife, cut an "X" in the center of the top crust; carefully fold back. Carefully pour butter mixture evenly into the pie; carefully replace top crust; leaving 4 vents, seal the rest of the pastry.
5. Place in preheated oven; bake for 30 minutes; remove from oven; set aside; reduce oven temperature to 325 degrees F.
6. Grate frozen butter into bowl; add flour, remaining sugars, remaining cinnamon and walnuts: carefully mix well.

7. Using foil, make a rim with a lip to hold nut topping and place around pie. Sprinkle nut topping evenly over top; return to oven; bake 30 to 40 minutes. Remove to wire rack to cool slightly.
8. Serve with ice cream, if desired.

Makes 1 pie.

About Ruby Tuesday:

This restaurant was formed in 1972, when Sandy Beall and four of his fraternity buddies from the University of Tennessee opened the first restaurant adjacent to the college campus in Knoxville. Today Ruby Tuesday® is one of three large public companies that dominate the bar-and-grill category of casual dining.

Ruby Tuesday Spicy Black Beans

Description: *A side dish of black beans in barbecue sauce.*

Ingredients

1 cup dry black beans
salt, to taste
1 small clove garlic, minced
1/4 cup onion, finely chopped
1/2 cup barbecue sauce

RecipeSecrets.net tip:
Save time by substituting canned black beans.

1. Place beans in colander; pick through to remove and stones; rinse well.

2. Transfer beans to medium-sized saucepan; add garlic, salt and onion; cover with 3 times the volume of water; bring to boil; cook, uncovered, 1 ½ to 2 hours or until beans are tender. If needed, add additional boiling water.

3. Drain beans in colander; transfer to microwaveable dish; add barbecue sauce; stir to blend well. Microwave on high for 1 minute or until heated through. This can be done in the oven as well. Combine beans and barbecue sauce; transfer to baking dish; bake in preheated 350 degree oven for 20 minutes or until heated through.

Makes about 2 cups.

Ruth's Chris Steak House Petite Filet

Description: *Tender cut filet steaks broiled to desired doneness and topped with fresh butter for a tantalizing experience.*

Ingredients

4 8-ounce filet mignon steaks   salt
5 tablespoons butter, softened   pepper
2 teaspoons chopped fresh parsley

1. Preheat broiler to high.
2. Place four ceramic oven-safe plates in the bottom of the broiler when you start to heat it up. Leave there while cooking filets.
3. Dry filets with a paper towel; rub ½ tablespoon butter over top and bottom of each steak; season with salt and pepper.
4. When broiler is hot (after 30 minutes of heating up), place a rack on the top so that when the filets are placed in the broiler they will be 5 to 6 inches from the heat. Cook filets in broiler pan, turning halfway through cooking time to desired doneness:

   - 4 to 6 minutes per side   Rare
   - 5 to 7 minutes per side   Medium Rare
   - 6 to 8 minutes per side   Medium
   - 6 to 9 minutes per side   Medium well
   - 10 to 11 minutes per side   Well

5. When meat is done, carefully remove plates from oven and place one tablespoon butter on each - it will sizzle and melt; place steak on dish; garnish with parsley.

Serves 4

About Ruth's Chris Steak House:

Famous for their signature steaks - seared to perfection and topped with fresh butter so they sizzle all the way to your table.

Ruth's Chris Steak House Sweet Potato Casserole

Description: *The good-old fashioned flavor or sweet potatoes topped with sweetened pecans.*

Ingredients

1 cup firmly packed brown sugar
1/3 cup flour
1 cup chopped pecans
1/2 stick butter, melted
3 cups cooked, mashed sweet
  potatoes
1 cup sugar
1/2 teaspoon salt
1 teaspoon vanilla

2 eggs, well beaten
1 stick (1/2 cup) butter, melted

1. Preheat oven to 350 degrees F.
2. Grease baking dish; set aside.
3. Prepare topping: Combine brown sugar, flour, nuts and melted butter; set aside.
4. In medium bowl, combine sweet potatoes, sugar, salt, vanilla, eggs and butter; mix well; transfer to prepared casserole. Cover evenly with topping.
5. Bake in preheated oven 30 minutes; allow to set for 15 minutes before serving.

Serves 6

Shoney's Broccoli Casserole

Description: *Broccoli and rice in a cheese sauce, topped with crushed crackers and more cheese.*

Ingredients

6 cups broccoli florets, coarsely chopped
1 1/4 lbs. Velveeta cheese
2 eggs
3 cups cooked rice
3 cups half and half
1 cup Ritz crackers, crushed

1 cup shredded Cheddar cheese
1/2 teaspoon salt
1/2 teaspoon black pepper
cooking spray

1. Preheat oven to 350 degrees F. Coat 9-inch baking pan with non-stick cooking spray; set aside.

2. In medium bowl, whisk eggs until well beaten; add broccoli florets, cooked rice, salt and pepper; mix well.

RecipeSecrets.net tip: Instead of microwaving, you can make the sauce in your double boiler.

3. Dice Velveeta into ¼-inch pieces and place in microwaveable container; Pour half-and-half over; cover and microwave on medium for 2 minutes or until cheese is melted. If desired, this can be done in the top of a double boiler over simmering water. Transfer to bowl with rice mixture; blend well.

4. Transfer mixture to baking pan. Place in preheated oven and bake for 30 minutes. Remove from oven, sprinkle with crushed crackers and cheddar cheese; return to oven and bake an additional 5 minutes or until cheese melts and cracker crumbs have browned.

Serves 6

Shoney's Strawberry Pie

Description: *The sweetness of fresh strawberries in a flaky crust.*

Ingredients

1 cup all purpose flour
1/4 teaspoon salt
3/8 cup butter
1 1/2 tablespoons shortening
1/8 cup ice water
red food coloring
fresh strawberries for garnish

Filling:
1 cup sugar
3 tablespoons corn starch
1 pint strawberries
12 ounces 7-UP
whipped cream

1. In medium bowl, add flour and salt; whisk to combine; using pastry cutter or 2 forks, cut in butter and shortening until mixture resembles coarse meal. Add water, a drop at a time; continue cutting until desired consistency for pie dough. Shape into ball; cover; chill for 1 hour.

2. Prepare filling. In medium-sized saucepan, combine sugar, cornstarch and 7-Up; whisk well. Cook over medium heat, stirring, until mixture becomes thick. Cool, to room temperature. Add a few drops of food coloring; mix well.

3. Preheat oven to 350 degrees F.

4. Remove dough from refrigerator and let stand 15 minutes before rolling. Pat dough into a round, roll to fit 9-inch pie pan. Crimp edges; place in preheated oven and bake shell until done; remove from oven and cool completely.

5. Wash and drain strawberries; cut into quarters, or smaller depending on size. Sprinkle with 1 or 2 teaspoons sugar; stir gently and transfer to cooled pie shell. Pour 7-Up mixture over strawberries; allow to set for 10 minutes; refrigerate.

6. To serve, top with whipped cream and place a fresh strawberry on top.

Makes 1 pie.

Sonic Drive-In Cranberry Limeade

Description: *A simple blend of lemon-lime soda and cranberry with an extra twist of lime.*

Ingredients

1 (12 ounce) can Sprite soda
1/4 cup cranberry juice
1/2 lime, cut into wedges

1. In 16-ounce glass, add ice until 2/3 of the glass is filled.
2. Pour cold Sprite over ice; squeeze lime juice (from lime wedges) over glass; drop lime wedges into glass.
3. Add cranberry juice to fill; serve with a straw.

Makes one 16-ounce drink

About Sonic Drive-In:

The first Sonic® was opened in Oklahoma, originally called the Top Hat. It now has several locations across America. Carhops with roller skates deliver the orders to your car.

Starbucks Lemon-Tipped Biscotti

Description: *An Italian favorite biscotti cookie with tips dipped in a lemon glaze.*

Ingredients

Biscotti:
6 tablespoons unsalted butter, at room temperature
1/2 cup granulated sugar
1 tablespoon grated lemon zest
2 large eggs
1 teaspoon vanilla extract
2 cups all-purpose flour
2 teaspoons baking powder

1/4 teaspoon salt
1 cup shelled pistachios, roasted and coarsely chopped

Lemon Icing:
2 cups sifted confectioners' sugar
1 teaspoon grated lemon zest
1/4 cup lemon juice

1. Preheat oven to 375 degrees F.
2. In large bowl, cream butter, sugar and lemon zest until light and fluffy; add eggs, one at a time, beating well after each addition; stir in vanilla.
3. In small bowl, whisk flour, baking powder and salt. Gradually add to creamed mixture, beating well.
4. Stir in nuts.
5. On a lightly floured work surface, divide dough in half.
6. Lightly flour each piece and shape into a log measuring about 1 ½-inches in diameter and 9-inches long.
7. Place logs about 3-inches apart on ungreased baking sheet. Shape each log by pressing gently to a thickness of ¾-inch and 3-inches wide.
8. Bake in preheated oven until lightly browned on top, about 20 minutes.
9. Cool 10 minutes on the pan, transfer to cutting board. Using a long, sharp knife, cut each log crosswise into ¾-inch thick slices.

10. Return cookies, cut side down, close together, to baking sheet. Return to hot oven and bake 10 minutes. Remove and turn cookies over to toast second side, baking an additional 10 minutes or until golden brown.

11. Transfer immediately to wire racks to cool completely.

12. Prepare icing in small bowl: Combine sugar, lemon zest and lemon juice; beat until smooth. Additional drops of lemon juice can be added for a consistency that will allow icing to coat cookies lightly. Dip one end of each cookie into the icing; turn to coat tip evenly; allow excess to drip off; place on wire rack until icing sets.

Makes about 2 1/2 dozen Biscotti.

Subway Chipotle Southwest Sauce

Description: *A smooth and spicy sauce with a kick for any of your favorite sandwiches, subs and hoagies. Makes a nice dip for your favorite dippers.*

Ingredients

1 cup mayonnaise
1/2 ounce Dijon mustard
1/2 ounce freshly squeezed lime juice
1 ounce chipotle chile in adobo, pureed
1/4 ounce fresh garlic, minced
salt, to taste

RecipeSecrets.net tip: This makes a nice salad dressing as well.

1. In small bowl, combine all ingredients; mix well.
2. Cover; refrigerate before using.

Makes about 1 cup.

About Subway:

Subway® is the world's largest submarine sandwich chain with more than 30,000 restaurants in 87 countries.

Taco Bell Hot Sauce

Description: *Their famous tomato-based hot sauce for your tacos, burritos, fajitas and more.*

Ingredients

6 oz. can tomato paste
3 cups water
2 teaspoons cayenne pepper
1 1/2 tablespoons chili powder
2 1/2 teaspoons salt
2 teaspoons cornstarch
2 teaspoons distilled white vinegar
1 tablespoons minced dried onion
2 tablespoons canned jalapeno slices

RecipeSecrets.net tip:
For a milder sauce, only use half of the cayenne and jalapeno

1. In medium saucepan, combine tomato paste and water; place over medium heat; stir until smooth.
2. Add cayenne pepper, chili powder, salt, cornstarch, vinegar and dried onion; stir to blend well.
3. Chop jalapeno slices very fine; add to saucepan.
4. Bring to boil; continue to stir; boil and stir for 3 minutes; remove from heat. Cool.
5. When cool, transfer to a container with a tight seal; refrigerate.

Makes about 3 cups.

T.G.I. Friday's Jack Daniels Grill Glaze

Description: *Their famous glaze for ribs, chicken, wings or fish - slightly sweet and slightly spicy.*

Ingredients

1 head garlic
1 tablespoon olive oil
2/3 cup water
1 cup pineapple juice
1/4 cup Kikkoman Teriyaki
Sauce
1 tablespoon soy sauce
1 1/3 cup dark brown sugar, firmly packed

3 tablespoons lemon juice
3 tablespoons minced white
onion
1 tablespoon Jack Daniels
Whiskey
1 tablespoon crushed pineapple
1/4 teaspoon cayenne pepper

1. Preheat oven to 350 degrees F.

2. Roast garlic: Peel away outer layers of garlic bulb skin, leaving the skins on the individual cloves intact. With a sharp knife, cut off ¼ to ½-inch from the top of the cloves to expose the individual cloves. Place in baking pan or in muffin tin (works great in muffin tin); drizzle with oil; rub with fingers to make sure the head is well coated; cover with foil and bake for 45 to 60 minutes, or until cloves feel soft when pressed.

3. Allow to cool enough so that you can touch it without burning yourself. Using a small knife, cut the skin slightly around each clove; squeeze cloves out of their skins or use a cocktail fork to remove.

4. In medium saucepan, combine water, pineapple juice, teriyaki sauce, soy sauce and brown sugar; place over medium-high heat and bring to a boil, stirring occasionally. Reduce heat to a simmer. Add remaining ingredients; stir to blend well.

5. Add 2 teaspoons roasted garlic to sauce; simmer for 35 to 45 minutes, or until sauce has reduced by half, is thick and has the consistency of syrup. Be careful that the sauce does not boil over.

Makes 1 cup

About T.G.I. Friday's:

T.G.I. Friday's®, one of the first American casual dining chains, is a dining experience that has become the favorite pastime of millions since 1965.The first T.G.I. Friday's was located at First Avenue and 63rd Street in New York City. Their focus is on providing a comfortable, relaxing environment where guests can enjoy quality food and have a good time.

T.G.I. Friday's Soy Dressing

Description: *Peanut oil and cider vinegar infused with the flavors of soy sauce, onion and honey with the added kick of hot mustard.*

Ingredients

1/3 cup peanut oil
1/3 cup cider vinegar
1/3 cup water
2 tablespoons soy sauce
2 tablespoons green onion stems
1 tablespoon honey
1/2 teaspoon prepared hot mustard

1. Place ingredients in jar with tight-fitting lid; shake to mix well.
2. Refrigerate until ready to use. Shake well before using.
3. Will keep 3 to 4 days in refrigerator.

Makes about 1 cup.

T.G.I. Friday's Strawberry Fields Salad

Description: *The crunch of fresh greens, topped with glazed pecans and glazed strawberries.*

Ingredients

Glazed Pecans:
1 cup chopped pecans
1/4 cup dark brown sugar, firmly packed
1 tablespoon water

Strawberry Glaze:
12 strawberries, sliced 1/4-inch thick
1/4 cup balsamic vinegar
1/4 cup granulated sugar

2 tablespoons water

Salad:
1 head red leaf lettuce
1 head romaine lettuce
6 ounces balsamic vinaigrette dressing
2 ounces shredded Parmesan cheese
cracked black pepper to serve

1. In small saucepan, combine all ingredients for glazed peanuts; heat until sugar is dissolved; remove from heat; set aside.
2. In medium bowl, combine strawberry glaze ingredients; set aside.
3. Chop lettuce into bite-sized pieces; transfer to large bowl; toss with vinaigrette and Parmesan.
4. Divide between 2 serving dishes; top with glazed pecans.
5. Strain strawberries; place on top of salad; sprinkle with cracked black pepper.

Serves 2

Tony Chachere's Famous Creole Seasoning

Description: *This is a great seasoning to use in any recipe calling for Creole Seasoning. Use on your meats, poultry, fish and vegetables.*

Ingredients

26 ounces salt, free flowing
1 1/2 ounces pepper, black, ground
2 ounces red peppers, ground
1 ounce garlic powder
1 ounce chili powder
1 ounce Accent seasoning

1. Combine ingredients; whisk well to combine.
2. Transfer to container with tight-fitting lid; store in pantry. Use like salt.

About Tony Chachere's:

Tony Chachere's Creole Foods began in 1972, following the success of Chachere's Cajun Country Cookbook. The company now offers a variety of cookbooks, seasoning blends, dinner mixes, marinades, sauces, batters, and frozen items that are prepared with Chachere's products.

Tony Roma's Original Barbecue Sauce

Description: *Not too spicy, but just the right kick.*

Ingredients

1 cup ketchup
1 cup vinegar
1/2 cup dark corn syrup
2 teaspoons sugar

1/2 teaspoon salt
1/4 teaspoon garlic powder
1/4 teaspoon onion powder
1/4 teaspoon Tabasco sauce

RecipeSecrets.net tip:
Add more Tabasco for some
added kick.

1. In saucepan, combine all ingredients; place over high heat; whisk to blend until smooth.
2. Bring mixture to boil; reduce heat; simmer, uncovered for about 35 minutes to thicken. If it gets to thick, thin with a bit of vinegar.

Makes about 1 cup of sauce.

About Tony Roma's:

Tony Roma's is a worldwide success story! Well known as the pioneer of Baby Back Ribs with their signature sauces and rib recipes that have won countless awards. At Tony Roma's, they are committed to providing you the best ribs anywhere. Using new rib styles and sauce flavors, their chefs are working hard to make Tony Roma's the only choice for ribs. But the Tony Roma's story does not end with ribs. Crispy fresh salads, mouth watering char-grilled steaks, their original BBQ chicken, and delicious seafood make up a menu that is sure to please every guest.

White Castle Burgers

Description: *White Castle is famous for their signature "Slyders"-steam grilled on a bed of onions and served with a pickle on a soft bun.*

Ingredients

12 dinner rolls (2 1/2" x 2 1/2" size)
1 pound lean ground beef
1/2 cup water (for beef)
1/2 teaspoon salt
3/4 cup diced onions
1 beef bouillon cube or 1 teaspoon beef bouillon granules
1/2 cup water (for onions)
dill pickle slices

1. Using food processor, process beef, salt and water to blend well. The meat should look a little pasty.
2. Line a 11 X 13-inch jelly roll pan with plastic wrap. Place beef mixture on plastic wrap and cover with another piece of plastic wrap. Roll out to 1/4-inch thickness. Remove plastic wrap and cut into 3 X 3-inch squares on a tray. Using a straw, poke 5 holes (like the 5 dots on a die) in each patty. These are the steam holes. Cover with plastic wrap and freeze until partially frozen.
3. Place onions, beef bouillon and ½ cup water in skillet and saute over low heat until onions are clear, adding more water if needed. Set aside.
4. When ready to cook patties, return pan of onions to medium low heat and add just enough water to the onions to cover the bottom of the pan. Add patties; cover with lid.
5. These cook quickly - turn and cook until done but not dry.

RecipeSecrets.net tip:
Add a slice of cheese for
cheeseburgers.

6. When done place on roll with pickles; cover to steam slightly or place
in the microwave for a few seconds.

Serves 4-6

About White Castle:

White Castle® White Castle has been in business for
over 80 years and has almost 400 locations. They
were the first fast food restaurant in existence selling
the first million and first billion burgers. They also
are the first to sell frozen fast food in supermarkets.

HELPFUL COOKING TIPS

1. Always chill juices or sodas before adding to beverage recipes.

2. Store ground coffee in the refrigerator or freezer to keep it fresh.

3. Seeds and nuts, both shelled and unshelled, keep best and longest when stored in the freezer. Unshelled nuts crack more easily when frozen. Nuts and seeds can be used directly from the freezer.

4. To prevent cheese from sticking to a grater, spray the grater with cooking spray before beginning.

5. Fresh lemon juice will remove onion scent from hands.

6. Instant potatoes are a good stew thickener.

7. Three large stalks of celery, chopped and added to about two cups of beans (navy, brown, pinto, etc.), will make them easier to digest.

8. When cooking vegetables that grow above ground, the rule of thumb is to boil them without a cover.

9. A scoop of sugar added to water when cooking greens helps vegetables retain their fresh color.

10. Never soak vegetables after slicing; they will lose much of their nutritional value.

11. To cut down on odors when cooking cabbage, cauliflower, etc..., add a little vinegar to the cooking water.

12. Perk up soggy lettuce by soaking it in a mixture of lemon juice and cold water.

13. Egg shells can be easily removed from hard-boiled eggs if they are quickly rinsed in cold water after they are boiled.

14. Keep bean sprouts and jicama fresh and crisp up to five days by submerging them in a container of water, then refrigerating them.

15. When trying to reduce your fat intake, buy the leanest cuts you can find. Fat will show up as an opaque white coating or can also run through the meat fibers, as marbling. Stay away from well-marbled

cuts of meat.

16. Pound meat lightly with a mallet or rolling pin, pierce with a fork, sprinkle lightly with meat tenderizer, and add marinade. Refrigerate for about 20 minutes, and you'll have tender meat.

17. Marinating is easy if you use a plastic bag. The meat stays in the marinade and it's easy to turn and rearrange.

18. It's easier to thinly slice meat if it's partially frozen.

19. Tomatoes added to roasts will help to naturally tenderize them.

20. Cut meats across the grain; they will be easier to eat and have a better appearance.

21. When frying meat, sprinkle paprika over it to turn it golden brown.

22. Always thaw all meats in the refrigerator for maximum safety.

23. Refrigerate poultry promptly after purchasing. Keep it in the coldest section of your refrigerator for up to two days. Freeze poultry for longer storage. Never leave poultry at room temperature for more than two hours.

24. If you're microwaving skinned chicken, cover the baking dish with vented clear plastic wrap to keep the chicken moist.

25. Lemon juice rubbed on fish before cooking will enhance the flavor and help maintain a good color.

26. Scaling a fish is easier if vinegar is rubbed on the scales first.

27. Over-ripe bananas can be peeled and frozen in a plastic container until it's time to bake bread or cake.

28. When baking bread, a small dish of water in the oven will help keep the crust from getting too hard or brown.

29. Use shortening to grease pans, as margarine and oil absorb more readily into the dough or batter (especially bread).

30. To make self-rising flour, mix 4 cups flour, 2 tea-

spoons salt, and 2 tablespoons baking powder, and store in a tightly covered container.

31. Hot water kills yeast. One way to tell the correct temperature is to pour the water over your forearm. If you cannot feel either hot or cold, the temperature is just right.

32. When in doubt, always sift flour before measuring.

33. When baking in a glass pan, reduce the oven temperature by 25 degrees.

34. When baking bread, you get a finer texture if you use milk. Water makes a coarser bread.

35. To make bread crumbs, toast the heels of bread and chop in a blender or food processor.

36. Cracked eggs should not be used as they may contain bacteria.

37. The freshness of eggs can be tested by placing them in a large bowl of cold water; if they float, do not use them.

38. Dust a bread pan or work surface with flour by filling an empty glass salt shaker with flour.

39. To slice meat into thin strips for stir-fry dishes, partially freeze it so it will be easier to slice.

40. To keep cauliflower white while cooking, add a little milk to the water.

41. A roast with the bone in will cook faster than a boneless roast. The bone carries the heat to the inside more quickly.

42. For a juicier hamburger, add a little cold water to the beef before grilling.

43. To freeze meatballs, place them on a cookie sheet until frozen. Transfer to plastic bags and return to the freezer.

44. When boiling corn, add sugar to the water instead of salt. The salt will toughen the corn.

45. To ripen tomatoes, put them in a brown paper bag in a dark pantry.

46. To keep celery crisp, stand it upright in a pitcher of cold, salted water and refrigerate.

47. When cooking cabbage, place a small tin cup or can

half full of vinegar on the stove near the cabbage. It will absorb the odor.

48. Potatoes soaked in salt water for 20 minutes before baking will bake more rapidly.

49. Let raw potatoes stand in cold water for at least a half-hour before frying in order to improve the crispness of French-fried potatoes. Dry potatoes completely before adding to oil.

50. A few drops of lemon juice in the water will whiten boiled potatoes.

51. Buy mushrooms before they "open."When stems and caps are attached firmly, they are fresh.

52. Do not use metal bowls when mixing salads. Use wood or glass.

53. Lettuce keeps better if you store it in the refrigerator without washing it. Keep the leaves dry. Wash the lettuce before using.

54. Never use soda to keep vegetables green. It destroys the Vitamin C.

55. If you over-salt your gravy, stir in some instant mashed potatoes to repair the damage. Add a little more liquid if necessary.

56. After stewing chicken, cool in broth before cutting to add more flavor.

COOKING TERMS

Au gratin: Topped with crumbs and/or cheese and browned in an oven or under a broiler.

Au jus: Served in its own juices.

Baste: To moisten foods during cooking with pan drippings or special sauce in order to add flavor and prevent drying.

Bisque: A thick cream soup.

Blanch: To immerse in rapidly boiling water and allow to cook slightly.

Cream: To soften a fat, like butter, by beating it at room temperature. Butter and sugar are often creamed together.

Crimp: To seal the edges of a two-crust pie either by pinching them at intervals with the fingers or a fork.

Crudites: An assortment of raw vegetables that is served as an hors d'oeuvre.

Degrease: To remove fat from the surface of stews and soups.

Dredge: To coat lightly with flour, cornmeal, bread crumbs, etc.

Entree: The main course.

Fold: To incorporate a delicate substance into another substance without releasing air bubbles.

Glaze: To cover with a glossy coating, such as a melted and diluted jelly for fruit desserts.

Julienne: To cut vegetables, fruits, or cheeses into match-shaped pieces.

Marinate: To allow food to stand in a liquid in order to tenderize or to add flavor.

Mince: To chop food into very small pieces.

Parboil: To boil until partially cooked; to blanch.

Pare: To remove the outer skin of a fruit or vegetable.

Poach: To cook gently in hot liquid kept just below the boiling point.

Saute: To cook food in a small amount of butter/oil.

Simmer: To cook in liquid just below the boiling point.

Steep: To let food stand in hot liquid in order to extract or enhance the flavor.

Toss: To combine ingredients with a repeated lifting motion.

Whip: To beat rapidly in order to incorporate air and produce expansion.

HERBS & SPICES

Basil: Sweet, warm flavor with an aromatic odor. Use whole or ground. Good with lamb, fish, roasts, stews, ground beef, vegetables, and dressings.

Bay Leaves: Pungent flavor. Use whole leaf but remove before serving. Good in vegetable dishes, seafood, stews and pickles.

Caraway: Spicy taste and aromatic smell. Use in cakes, breads, soups, cheese and sauerkraut.

Chives: Sweet, mild flavor like that of onion. Excellent in salads, fish, soups and potatoes.

Cilantro: Use fresh. Great in salads, salsa, fish, chicken, rice, beans and other Mexican dishes.

Curry Powder: Spices are combines to proper proportions to give a distinct flavor to meat, poultry, fish and vegetables.

Dill: Both seeds and leaves are flavorful. Leaves may be used as a garnish or cooked with fish, soup, dressings, potatoes, and beans. Leaves or the whole plant may be used to flavor pickles.

Fennel: Sweet, hot flavor. Both seeds and leaves are used. Use in small quantities in pies and baked goods. Leaves can be boiled with fish.

Ginger: A pungent root, this aromatic spice is sold fresh, dried, or ground. Use in pickles, preserves, cakes, cookies, and meat dishes.

Marjoram: May be used both dried or green. Use to

flavor fish, poultry, omelets, lamb, stew, stuffing and tomato juice.

Mint: Aromatic with a cool flavor. Excellent in beverages, fish, lamb, cheese, soup, peas, carrots and fruit desserts.

Oregano: Strong and aromatic. Use whole or ground in tomato juice, fish, eggs, pizza, chili, poultry, vegetables.

Paprika: A bright red pepper, this spice is used in meat, vegetables and soups or as a garnish for potatoes, salads or eggs.

Parsley: Best when used fresh, but can be used dried. Try in fish, omelets, soup, meat and mixed greens.

Rosemary: Very aromatic. Can be used fresh or dried. Season fish, stuffing, beef, lamb, poultry, onions, and potatoes.

Saffron: Orange-yellow in color, this spice flavors or colors foods. Use in soup, chicken, rice and breads.

Sage: Use fresh or dried. The flowers are sometimes used in salads. May be used in fish, beef, poultry, cheese spreads and breads.

Tarragon: Leaves have a pungent, hot taste. Use to flavor sauces, salads, fish, poultry, tomatoes, eggs, green beans and dressings.

Thyme: Sprinkle leaves on fish or poultry before broiling or baking. Add a few sprigs directly on coals shortly before meat is finished grilling.

ARE YOUR HERBS & SPICES FRESH?

Ingredient Shelf Life:

- Ground Spices 2-3 years
- Whole Spices 3-4 years
- Seasoning Blends 1-2 years
- Herbs 1-3 years
- Extracts 4 years, except pure vanilla, which lasts forever

Still not sure, then use these guidelines:

- Check to see that the color of your spices and herbs is vibrant.

- If the color has faded, chances are so has the flavor.

- Rub or crush the spice or herb in your hand. If the aroma is weak and flavor is not apparent, it's time to replace it.

- Store herbs and spices in a tightly capped container, and keep away from heat, moisture, and direct sunlight. Replace bottle lids tightly immediately after use.

- To minimize moisture and caking, use a dry measuring spoon and avoid sprinkling directly into a steaming pot.

- Check the freshness date on the container.

GUIDELINES FOR BUYING FRESH VEGETABLES

Artichokes: Look for compact, tightly closed heads with green, clean-looking leaves. Avoid those with leaves that are brown or separated.

Asparagus: Stalks should be tender and firm; tips should be close and compact. Choose the stalks with very little white; they are more tender. Use asparagus soon after purchasing because it toughens rapidly.

Beans: Those with small seeds inside the pods are best. Avoid beans with dry-looking pods.

Broccoli, Brussels Sprouts, Cauliflower: Flower clusters on broccoli and cauliflower should be tight and close together. Brussels sprouts should be firm and compact. Smudgy, dirty spots may indicate pests or disease.

Cabbage and Head Lettuce: Choose heads that are heavy for their size. Avoid cabbage with worm holes and lettuce with discoloration or soft rot.

Cucumbers: Choose long, slender cucumbers for best quality. Avoid yellow ones.

Mushrooms: Caps should be closed around the stems. Avoid black or brown gills.

Peas and Lima Beans: Select pods that are well-filled but not bulging. Avoid dried, spotted, yellow, or flabby pods.

GUIDELINES FOR BUYING FRESH FRUITS

Bananas: Skin should be free of bruises and black or brown spots. Purchase green and allow them to ripen at home at room temperature.

Berries: Select plump, solid berries with good color. Avoid stained containers which indicate wet or leaky berries. Berries without clinging caps, such as black-berries and raspberries, may be unripe. Strawberries without caps may be overripe.

Melons: In cantaloupes, thick, close netting on the rind indicates best quality. Cantaloupes are ripe when the stem scar is smooth and the space between the net-ting is yellow or yellow-green. They are best when fully ripe with fruity odor. Honeydews are ripe when rind has creamy to yellowish color and velvety tex-ture. Immature honeydews are whitish-green. Ripe watermelons have some yellow color on one side. If melons are white or pale green on one side, they are not ripe.

Oranges, Grapefruit and Lemons: Choose those heavy for their size. Smoother, thinner skins usually indicate more juice. Most skin markings do not affect quality. Oranges with a slight greenish tinge may be just as ripe as fully colored ones. Light or greenish-yellow lemons are more tart than deep yellow ones. Avoid citrus fruits showing withered, sunken or soft areas.

MEASUREMENTS

a pinch	1/8 teaspoon or less
3 teaspoons	1 tablespoon
4 tablespoons	1/4 cup
8 tablespoons	1/2 cup
12 tablespoons	3/4 cup
16 tablespoons	1 cup
2 cups	1 pint
4 cups	1 quart
4 quarts	1 gallon
8 quarts	1 peck
4 pecks	1 bushel
16 ounces	1 pound
32 ounces	1 quart
1 ounce liquid	2 tablespoons
8 ounces liquid	1 cup

Use standard measuring cups and spoons.

All measurements are level.

RECIPES BY CATEGORY

Salads

Side Dishes

Miscellaneous

TRADEMARKS

- Applebee's is a registered trademark of Applebee's International, Inc.
- Aunt Jemima is a registered trademark of The Quaker Oats Company.
- B.B. King's Blues Club & Restaurant is a registered trademark of B.B. King Blues Club & Grill.
- Bahama Breeze is a registered trademark of Darden Concepts, Inc.
- Bailey's is a registered trademark of R&A Bailey & Co.
- Balducci's is a registered trademark of Balducci's.
- Ben & Jerry's is a registered trademark of Ben & Jerry's Homemade Holdings, Inc.
- Benihana is a registered trademark of Benihana, Inc.
- Black Eyed Pea is a registered trademark of Restaurants Acquisition 1, LLC.
- Bob Evans is a registered trademark of Bob Evans Farms Inc.
- Bob's Big Boy is a registered trademark of Big Boy Restaurants International, LLC.
- Bull's Eye is a registered trademark of Kraft Foods.
- Cajun Cafe is a registered trademark of Razzoo's Cajun Cafe.
- California Pizza Kitchen is a registered trademark of California Pizza Kitchen, Inc.
- Carl's Jr is a registered trademark of Carl Karcher Enterprises, Inc.
- Carrabba's is a registered trademark of OSI Restaurant Partners, LLC
- The Cheesecake Factory is a registered trademark of The Cheesecake Factory, Inc
- Chick-Fil-A is a registered trademark of CFA Properties, Inc.
- Chili's is a registered trademark of Brinker International.

- Chipotle Mexican Grill is a registered trademark of Chipotle Mexican Grill, Inc.
- Church's is a registered trademark of Cajun Operating Company.
- Claim Jumper is registered trademark of Claim Jumper Restaurant LLC
- Cracker Barrel is a registered trademark of CBOCS Properties, Inc.
- Dave & Buster's is a registered trademark of Dave & Buster's.
- Denny's is a registered trademark of DFO, LLC.
- El Torito's is a registered trademark of El Torito Restaurants, Inc.
- Emeril is a registered trademark of B&G Foods.
- Famous Dave's is a registered trademark of Famous Dave's of America, Inc.
- Girl Scout is a registered trademark of Girl Scouts of the United States of America.
- Golden Corral is a registered trademark of Golden Corral Corporation.
- Hard Rock Café is a registered trademark of Hard Rock America, Inc.
- Hardees is a registered trademark of Hardees Food Systems, Inc.
- Houlihan's is a registered trademark of Houlihan's Restaurants, Inc.
- Ikea is a registered trademark of Inter IKEA Systems B.V.
- Jack In The Box is a registered trademark of Jack In The Box Inc.
- Jiffy Mix is a registered trademark of Chelsea Milling Co.
- Jimmy Buffett's Margaritaville Restaurant is a regis-tered trademark of Margaritaville Cafe.
- Joe's Crab Shack is a registered trademark of Landry's Seafood Restaurants, Inc.
- Kenny Rogers Roasters is a registered trademark of Kenny Rogers Roasters.

- KFC, Pizza Hut,Taco Bell, and Long John Silver's are registered trademarks of Yum! Brands, Inc.
- Lawry's is a registered trademark of Lawry's Foods, LLC
- Little Caesar is a registered trademark of Little Caesar Enterprises, Inc.
- Long John Silver is a registered trademark of Yum! Brands, Inc.
- Macaroni Grill is a registered trademark of Brinker International.
- McDonald's and the Big Mac are trademarks of McDonald's Corporation.
- Michael Jordan's Steakhouse is a registered trademark of The Glazier Group.
- Mrs. Fields is a registered trademark of Mrs. Fields Gifts, Inc.
- Old Bay is a registered trademark of OLD BAY, Inc.
- Olive Garden is a registered trademark of Darden Restaurants, Inc.
- Outback Steakhouse is a registered trademark of Outback Steakhouse, Inc.
- Pappadeaux Seafood Kitchen is a registered trademark of PRI.
- Perkins Family Restaurant is a registered trademark of The Restaurant Company of Minnesota.
- Pizza Hut is a registered trademarks of Yum! Brands, Inc.
- P.F. Chang is a registered trademark of P.F. Chang's China Bistro, Inc.
- Planet Hollywood is a registered is a registered trademark of Planet Hollywood, Inc.
- Red Lobster is a registered trademark of Darden Restaurants, Inc.
- Red Robin is a registered trademark of Red Robin International, Inc.
- Ruby Tuesday is a registered trademark of Morrison Restaurants, Inc.

- Ruth's Chris Steak House is a registered trademark of Ruth's Hospitality Group, Inc.
- Shoney's is a registered trademark of Shoney's, Inc.
- Sonic Drive-In is a registered trademark of America's Drive-In Brand Properties LLC.
- Starbucks is a registered trademark of Starbucks Corporation.
- Subway is a registered trademark of Doctor's Associates Inc.
- Taco Bell is a registered trademarks of Yum! Brands, Inc.
- T.G.I. Friday's is a registered trademark of T.G.I. Friday's, Inc.
- Tony Chachere's is a registered trademark of Tony Chachere's.
- Tony Roma's is a registered trademark of Tony Roma's, Inc.
- White Castle is a registered trademark of White Castle Management Co.

To find a restaurant near you, please visit:

Applebee's	www.applebees.com
Aunt Jemima	www.auntjemima.com
B.B. King's Blues Cub	www.bbkingblues.com
Bahama Breeze	www.bahamabreeze.com
Bailey's	www.baileys.com
Balducci's	www.balduccis.com
Ben & Jerry's	www.benjerry.com
Benihana	www.benihana.com
Black Eyed Pea	www.theblackeyedpea.com
Bob Evans	www.bobevans.com
Bob's Big Boy	www.bigboy.com
California Pizza Kitchen	www.cpk.com
Carl's Jr.	www.carlsjr.com
Carraba's Italian Grill	www.carrabbas.com
Cheesecake Factory	www.thecheesecakefactory.com
Chick-Fil-A	www.chick-fil-a.com
Chili's	www.chilis.com
Chipotle Mexican Grill	www.chipotle.com
Church's	www.churchs.com
Claim Jumper	www.claimjumper.com
Cracker Barrel	www.crackerbarrel.com
Dave & Buster's	www.daveandbusters.com
Denny's	www.dennys.com
El Torito's	www.eltorito.com
Famous Dave's	www.famousdaves.com
Golden Coral	www.goldencorral.com
Hard Rock Cafe	www.hardrockcafe.com
Hardee's	www.hardees.com
Ikea	www.ikea.com
Jack In The Box	www.jackinthebox.com
Joe's Crab Shack	www.joescrabshack.com
Kenny Rogers Roasters	www.kennyrogers.cc
KFC	www.kfc.com
Little Caesar	www.littlecaesars.com
Long John Silver's	www.ljsilvers.com
Macaroni Grill	www.macaronigrill.com
McDonald's	www.mcdonalds.com
Michael Jordan Restaurants	www.mjrestaurants.com

Olive Garden — www.olivegarden.com
Outback Steakhouse — www.outback.com
Pappadeaux — www.pappadeaux.com
Perkins Family Restaurant — www.perkinsrestaurants.com
P.F. Chang's — www.pfchangs.com
Pizza Hut — www.pizzahut.com
Planet Hollywood — www.planethollywood.com
Red Lobster — www.redlobster.com
Red Robin — www.redrobin.com
Ruby Tuesday — www.rubytuesday.com
Ruth's Chris Steakhouse — www.ruthschris.com
Shoney's — www.shoneys.com
Sonic Drive-In — www.sonicdrivein.com
Starbucks — www.starbucks.com
Subway — www.subway.com
Taco Bell — www.tacobell.com
T.G.I. Friday's — www.fridays.com
Tony Roma's — www.tonyromas.com
White Castle — www.whitecastle.com

Recipe Favorites